T'ai Chi Chuan

D1795367

The book
This book transmits an understanding of the practice of T'ai Chi Chuan as a vital meeting ground of Eastern and Western thought. The symbolism of the individual movement figures offers meaningful perspectives for everyday life. The author presents a vivid explanation of how the brain steers personal thoughts, feelings and acts and how these processes can be influenced by the movement meditation, T'ai Chi Chuan.

The author
What is the human essence? What do people have in common and what makes them different from one another? How do people remain healthy? What are the requirements that enable the development and experience of full creative potential? These are the key questions that have guided the author throughout her life, motivating her to become a highschool teacher (1972), a T'ai Chi Chuan instructor of the long form, Yang style, according to Gerda Geddes (1988), and finally, to take a Master of Science degree as a psychologist (1998). These questions were the major influence on her professional and private activities of schoolteaching, teaching courses in adult education in Switzerland and the USA, counselling children and adults in the practice of healthcare, raising two children and studying psychology, the neuro-sciences and the science of religion. During the past 40 years Theresia Buser-Rüther has developed teaching programs, learning methods and educational material for students, teachers and parents. Her enthusiasm for critical, scientific reflection, which is accompanied by a delight in experimenting with the creation of new resources, has played a major part in her daily life until the present time.

www.taichi-healthcare.ch
www.taichi-gesundheitspflege.ch

To my family

Theresia Buser-Rüther

T'ai Chi Chuan

Movement and Meditation

Translated by Cary Rick

Bibliographic information of the German National Library
(Deutsche Nationalbibliothek)
The German National Library lists this publication in the German National
Bibliography; detailed bibliographic data can be called off from the Internet via
http://dnb.d-nb.de

Cover illustration: The Jade Maiden with distaff and fan – a small figurine, private
property, photo © Theresia Buser-Rüther

© 2010 Theresia Buser-Rüther
Cover design, composition, production and publishing house:
Books on Demand GmbH, Norderstedt

ISBN 978-3-8334-7136-0

Inhalt

Foreword

Historic movement phenomena are, by nature, ephemeral artifacts. Since they are passed on from one person to the next through imitation, by the time the contemporary researcher turns to them, the vagaries of memory, personal physical capabilities, individual interests, or fashion have, by force of nature, taken liberties with their original structures. What does survive undoubtedly represents something characteristic about the movement phenomenon in question, but its legibility as a movement text, however, can only be approached through in-depth study and interpretation. By localizing the determinant cultural aspects that prevailed at the time of its initial conception and reception, the movement artifact can be reinstated and seen within the reality context of its original environment.

T'ai Chi Chuan is a succession of prescribed movement figures promoting the mutual well being of body and mind. Although its antecedents probably date back to the pre-Christian era in ancient China, these movement elements seem to have undergone a process of codification as training for the martial arts that began in the 13th century and culminated at the beginning of the 19th century. Since the thoroughly formalized character of its pre-fixed spatial and gestural choreography allows little or no room for improvisation, and historically authentic, detailed description offers instructions on how these movements are to be physically executed, T'ai Chi Chuan might today well resemble its original form to a high degree. Widely popularized throughout China, it is still practiced as a daily ritual by millions of inhabitants. On account of an interest in holistic eastern practices in the United States and Europe in the aftermath of the Second World War, T'ai Chi Chuan, along with Yoga, became available as "new age" calisthenics.

The movement approaches of T'ai Chi Chuan and Yoga differ entirely. Whereas T'ai Chi Chuan is especially concerned with the way a movement relates to the surrounding space, this does not play a significant role in Yoga at all. The movement exercises in Yoga strive to gain control over the body itself; T'ai Chi Chuan does not aim at a mastery of the body, but, through a cultivation of balanced effort, a mastery of its movements in relation to space. In contrast to the procedure in T'ai Chi Chuan, Yoga exercises need not be all executed at the same session, nor is it necessary to execute them in any prescribed order.

T'ai Chi Chuan, Yang style, seems to have proceeded toward formal standardization between the beginning of the 19th century and the onset of the Second World War in the 20th century. This time slot corresponds with the ultimate artistic flowering of Chinese opera between 1830 and 1960 in the celebrated productions of the Peking opera. Do the traditional gestures, postures and spatial displacements of the actors in the Chinese opera serve as a reference for the movements in T'ai Chi Chuan? With origins dating back to the Tang dynasty (712 – 755), the Chinese opera is also rooted deeply in ancient Chinese culture. Its theatrical procedure is formalized to the point of extreme stylisation. The prescribed way the actors are to conduct themselves in movement, was also passed down, like the movement figures in T'ai Chi Chuan, by imitation from generation to generation. It was not until the 20th century that librettos were written down at all. But even though Peking opera productions also included the scenic glimpses of the martial arts, T'ai Chi Chuan is not, nor ever was, intended to be accessed through the observation of movement. Its approach focuses exclusively on the personal movement experience of the practitioner himself.

Theresia Buser-Rüther approaches the historical context of T'ai Chi Chuan by investigating the meanings of the traditional designations of each of its movement figures. Within this context, each designation reveals its corresponding movements as the physical formulation of a Taoistic insight. The presentation of these findings brings the designation of a particular movement figure to mind, the legendary "Jade Maiden", a sort of Chinese patron saint of the craft of spinning and weaving. In this book the motifs that constitute the fabric of T'ai Chi Chuan are like colored threads that appear, disappear and re-appear in the weave. The author spins these threads from a variety of sources, that range from neurobiology and psychology on the one hand, and Taoism on the other, passing along the way through pertinent aspects of ancient Chinese culture, such as myth, shamanistic belief and alchemy.

The practice of T'ai Chi Chuan aims at achieving and maintaining self-composure through the detachment from affect. The idea of transcending individual emotional preoccupations with worldly cares in order that personal conduct be governed by ethical, moral or philosophical principles instead of self-concern, is not unusual. All religions, for example, apply this very same strategy. What does make T'ai Chi Chuan an uncommon movement artifact, however, is that the principle insights it conveys are embodied in the very movement figures themselves. T'ai Chi Chuan approaches body movement as a medium capable of generating an abstraction of personal existence. The immediate experience of moving through its succession of figures functions as the path of enlightenment, or – to put that in Taoistic terms – the enlightenment of the path. Within this context, enlightenment is not the result of movement experience; it is the movement experience itself. Ascribing this particular potential to body movement is a unique feature of T'ai Chi Chuan.

Theresia Buser-Rüther explores and explains the specific synthesis of cultural and neurobiological components that constitutes T'ai Chi Chuan's effectiveness as a meditative practice. Along the way, the form and content of T'ai Chi Chuan seem to be bearing movement testimony to an entire civilization.

Cary Rick, movement analyst

Toward T'ai Chi Chuan

While living in Baltimore, Maryland, in 1986, I came across leaflets advertising T'ai Chi Chuan in a center for alternative medicine and organic foods. This was the first description of the Chinese movement art I had ever read, and it intrigued me. I was fascinated by the idea of slow movements that could simultaneously promote the health of body and mind. Shortly after returning home to Switzerland I noticed that a course was being held not far from where I lived. I signed up and met, thus, my T'ai Chi teacher, Judy Schünemann-Sharpe, who lived in London. In her class I immediately felt the benevolent effect of the movements, which seemed, moreover, tailor-made for my physical resources. Three years of intensive training followed.

Judy Schünemann's teaching built on the insights of her teacher, Gerda Geddes, who had spent ten years in China where she learned the long form of T'ai Chi Chuan, Yang style. Geddes brought this form back to London's Centre for Contemporary Dance, "The Place", where she was to teach it for many years. Alongside movement work, Gerda Geddes turned toward Chinese literary texts and her knowledge of psychoanalysis in order to examine the symbolism of the names of the separate movement figures. Most schools of T'ai Chi Chuan today refer to these names as purely formal indications without further meaning. As it happens, much of the ancient knowledge about them was, indeed, lost during the Cultural Revolution.

Gerda Geddes achieved some renown in England during the 1970's and 80's. A television broadcast focused on her work, a film was made and she published a book, "Looking for the Golden Needle. An allegorical journey." By pointing out the coherency of the symbol as the link between physical training and spiritual insight Geddes developed a new approach to holistic well-being. This approach also corresponded entirely, toward the end of the twentieth century, with the spirit of the times. Gerda

Geddes' way of teaching was echoed in Judy Schünemann's classes, who mentioned now and again that further research was needed, in order to develop Geddes' frequently intuitive insights. This was tempting.

In 1991 I began work on a second degree in psychology, neuroscience, and the science of religion at the University of Zurich, where I was licensed in 1998 (today: Master of Science). The knowledge I acquired opened up a uniquely broad field of research to explore the perspectives Gerda Geddes had established. This resulted in several research projects that correlated the practice of T'ai Chi Chuan with various psychological, neurobiological and religious phenomena. One religious-scientific study explored the relationship between Chinese creation myths and child development. An image of Pan Gu, a spirit of creation in ancient Chinese mythology, revealed a surprising association with T'ai Chi Chuan. New avenues of thought offered by the research of Professor Norbert Bischof, helped me gain a greater understanding of the move, "Hold the circle" which is repeated again and again in T'ai Chi Chuan. In the course of this research I discovered myths, fairy tales and illustrations that further enriched the traditional names of the moves with contents simultaneously meaningful for body, mind and spirit.

During an examination of Chinese alchemy, I came across pre-Christian sources that offered insights about the development of T'ai Chi Chuan. Depth psychologist C.G. Jung's essays on alchemy in the Middle East and Europe encouraged a comparison with Chinese alchemy. Here I was to rediscover the T'ai Chi Chuan image of the snake that transforms itself into a golden bird. It is an ancient symbol for a developmental process of the psyche, in which new perspectives enter into consciousness. Human development is always concerned with creation. Since, from an individual point of view, every moment is a new experience, human development can be seen as an ongoing creative act. Generating such moments all by oneself is a pleasure and a process that affects the self-understanding and the world-view of the creator.

My studies were focused on correlations of body, mind and spirit. A connection came about between research on creativity and neuroscience in the 90's, when I had the good fortune to find in Martha Koukkou-Lehmann a professor, who had very early on begun research on the interrelation of feeling and thought. Her model of cerebral function guided my neuroscientific approach to T'ai Chi Chuan.

I am grateful to Professor Fritz Stolz, who, sadly, died much too soon. He made it possible for me to do a comprehensive religious-scientific examination of various Eastern and Western forms of meditation. In this research I applied different scientific concepts and models of psychology and neuroscience in order to compare T'ai Chi Chuan with Za-Zen, a Christian form of meditation, transcendental meditation, and some relaxation techniques that had evolved in a medical context. This comparative study resulted in the development of a model for indicating changes of perception through meditation.

Professor Jianxiang Rong from Nanking, China, astronomer and T'ai Chi Chuan practitioner, enabled me to gain access to a wealth of enriching source materials. Many thanks go to him for his support. The documents, which included teaching videos, books, images, stories, figures and textiles concerning T'ai Chi Chuan, create a concrete reference to both the old and the new Chinas that vivifies research and practice.

While working on the study I organized courses for Judy Schünemann three or four times a year in my own atelier. Inbetween her visits, my own teaching practice gave me the opportunity to develop teaching procedures that drew on my own insights into brain research and cognitive psychology.

Current neuro-scientific and psychological research affirms the holistic approach to T'ai Chi Chuan as applicable knowledge. The fundamentals of my own work rest on the correlation of these different scientific approaches. T'ai Chi is a source of inspiration that renews itself repeatedly, for it can be practiced at any age, in any situation, anyplace, without equipment, and it promotes health even when being used as purely mental training.

During the course of many years teaching T'ai Chi, I was also transposing the results of my research at the university into a language accessible to the layman in order to offer the participants in my courses written supplements to their classes. Their positive resonance to my holistic approach to body, mind and spirit became the motivation for this book. It aims at being useful to any practitioner, no matter the particular form, by offering information regarding psychology, brain research, the science of religion, and references to texts and images that serve a holistic approach to T'ai Chi.

My biggest thanks go to those people who came to my classes. They were ever-present in my mind's eye while I was writing. This helped me evolve a written form that is, on the one hand, generally intelligible, without, on the other hand, sacrificing critical, scientific accuracy. Heartfelt thanks go to Elisabeth Altorfer, for her studious examination of the manuscript, and for multi-faceted discussions about the application of scientific perspectives in everyday life. My husband, Roland Buser, did the editorial work on this book. Loving thanks go to him for his critical perusal. This book has found an informed and sensitive translator in movement analyst Cary Rick. Warm thanks go to him for his painstaking work.

My fascination with T'ai Chi Chuan began in the practical training of my teacher, Judy Schünemann-Sharpe, who introduced me to the particular interpretation of Gerda Geddes. I would like to thank her for this here. Later, my enthusiasm found scientific footing during my university studies and it continues to grow today in every class I teach and every time I practice T'ai Chi. I hope the reader finds as much enjoyment in this book as I did while writing it. Or, to put the above into two symbolic terms of T'ai Chi Chuan: With this book I "open the fan" and "shoot the golden arrow".

Part I

Fundamentals

T'ai Chi Chuan has a distinct aesthetic significance for the practitioner, as well as the observer. Although just twenty years ago the sight of a T'ai Chi group moving together out of doors somewhere seemed odd, people have become more accustomed to it today. Yet since the slowness of the moves still seems strange to many, they question its sense, its practical use and/or its origins. The following chapters offer access to the fundamentals of T'ai Chi Chuan. Their historical, philosophical and physiological backgrounds disclose the profound coherence of body, mind and spirit that is its core.

Historical background

The origins of T'ai Chi Chuan are not entirely certain. Many references in ancient Chinese Literature, such as images or instructions for gymnastic exercises seem to relate to T'ai Chi Chuan, as we know it today. Illustrations of physical exercises dating back, in part, to the third century B.C. reveal figures in body positions similar to those found in T'ai Chi Chuan.[1] Drawings and texts inscribed on silk that were found in Taoist graves dating from B.C. 168 thematize techniques of breathing, or stretching and bending, and also bear designations that include references to animals, like "roaming bear" or "stretching bird". Young and old people, as well as men and women are portrayed here.[2] Instructions for preventative health measures addressed to the general population can be found in "Thai-Chhing Tao Yin Yang Shêng Shing" (Manual for the Cultivation of Vitality through Physical Exercise and Self-massage) either from the Tang period, or perhaps during the flourishing culture of the early Sung period (between 600 and 1000 A.D.). These also relate to fundamentals of T'ai Chi Chuan.[3]

It is reported, that the Taoist monk Chang San-Feng (1279 – 1368) founded a so-called "internal school of boxing". He was a master of the "external" Shaolin-school, training center for martial art that was a part of the most famous monastery in China. He questioned the harshness of boxing and the exercise of brute force. It is told, that one day he observed a fight between a crane and a snake, in which the supple, flowing movements of the snake enabled it, on the one hand, to repeatedly evade the pointed attacks of the bird and, on the other hand, make surprise attacks. The crane stopped moving always and again, in order to be able to take aim. In these moments of immobility, the crane had exposed its Achilles heel, and the snake won. On account of this observation Chang San-Feng's teaching emphasized the need for gentleness and yielding while fighting. One was supposed to follow the movements of the opponent without losing balance and, through one's own ability to yield, induce his loss of balance and gain the upper hand. This story demonstrates the Taoist idea of the dynamic delicacy of the process of change. Suppleness of movement, whether physical, spiritual or social, is advantageous and promotes health. This link between Taoist thought and physical exercise is rooted very far back in Chinese history.

As we know it today, T'ai Chi Chuan in the Yang style is accredited to Yang Lu Chan (1799 – 1872) who taught the emperor and groups in public places. Yang Chen Fu (1883 – 1936), one of his grandchildren, established the Yang school. In time, this form spread throughout China and, from the 1950s, to the West. During the past 150 years the Yang style has proved a fertile ground for countless variations. Not only can long or short forms be learned, other versions include the use of poles, swords or fans. Different styles, such as Chen, Sun, or Wu contain further variations.

The long form of the Yang style used by Gerda Geddes corresponds to a great degree with the standardized version of the International T'ai Chi Chuan Association (ITCCA). By including the reflection of the designations of the movement figures as symbols, however, Geddes' version features a Western innovation. This was, in part, an outcome of her personal life experience.

Gerda Geddes grew up in Norway where, during long hikes with her grandfather, she developed an intense relationship with nature. Experiencing herself as a part of nature, adapting to it and learning from it, became major aspects of her self-understanding. Later, Geddes studied psychology and dance in the United States, and she also undertook Reichian psychoanalysis. When she was 41, she traveled with her family to China, where, during her ten-year stay, she came into contact with T'ai Chi Chuan and studied with two masters. The references to animals contained in the traditional names of the separate movement figure fascinated Geddes from the outset. These names were considered to be purely superficial orientation aids and are, indeed, still taught as such in most schools. After she had returned to England, and was convalescing after a long illness, Geddes turned toward Chinese literature and came upon a wealth of references relating to the names of the separate movement figures that mentioned animals. She was preoccupied as well with the theories of C. G. Jung and with "I Ching, The Book of Changes", one of the oldest books of wisdom in human history with roots that go back 3000 years in the history of Chinese culture. The references Geddes discovered permitted her to interpret contents that were symbolized in the names of the separate movement figures. The Jungian concept of archetypes motivated her to appraise those symbols in T'ai Chi that cut across cultural boundaries and can also be meaningful for Westerners. In 1962, at the age of 55, she began to transmit her findings by teaching at "the Place", a school for Modern Dance, through televised demonstrations, by publishing a book and distributing videotaped documentations. Her students also propagated her work in Europe, which brought about further modifications of the form of T'ai Chi Chuan she had evolved. But Geddes herself welcomed change. The Taoist concept of change, that she saw materialized in T'ai Chi Chuan, rejects the unswerving adherence to a fixed scheme, for fixation proves itself to be impractical. In this sense, one could imagine new forms of T'ai Chi, for example, for people suffering from arthritis, and for whom particular rotations and bending motions can be particularly painful. The great freedom that Gerda Geddes accorded to the needs of individual participants differs from the practice of other schools that hold fast to tradition and only allow for modifications when an experienced master presents them. Geddes' approach to T'ai Chi Chuan is typically Western, for she decodes its symbols through depth psychology.

Neuro-science opens another avenue of understanding of T'ai Chi Chuan. Current neuro-biological research that, like depth psychology, is rooted in Western culture, confirms the body-mind link that is manifest in Geddes' depth-psychological deliberations. They further the explanation of why T'ai Chi promotes relaxation and health.

Philosophical background

T'ai Chi Chuan rests on a philosophical fundament closely related to Taoism. Its symbol, Yin and Yang – ☯ – which is often used for T'ai Chi as well, represents the life forces Yin (feminine) and Yang (masculine) which are both enclosed within the same circle. The light component is masculine and contains a dark feminine component. The dark feminine component contains a light masculine component. Both components curve to fit closely into one another and signify perpetual motion.

The world view of the ancient Taoists is dualistic: Two forces, masculine and feminine, are in constant interaction, influence each other, oppose each other, complete each other. Subjected to this play of forces, all human beings and the world are in a state of perpetual change. These fundamental principles are present in every manifestation of nature, in every human being, in every community, every undertaking. Furthermore, in contrast to the Western notion that progress is always striving forward[4], Taoism conceives progress as movements backward and forward within a circle or sphere as portrayed in the Yin-Yang symbol. The Taoist never abandons the circle, but tries, with forwards and backwards movements, to fill it entirely, sensing its boundaries attentively while simultaneously maintaining the consciousness of his own center. This simultaneous presence in the circle and in one's own center enables the experience of a depth that compares, in a Taoist image, to water, whose nature it is to fill the deepest cavity before flowing on.

In T'ai Chi Chuan the repetition of the movement "Hold the Circle", reminds one to remain aware, in every moment of life of one's own center. Stepping forwards or backwards through a slow, progressive shift of weight along the sole of the foot makes one aware of one's own center and of the constant change to which one is subjected. The way the center is relating to movements of the foot or the arms enables the maintenance of balance.

Change is the essence of movement. Whereas Taoism observes the workings of this principle in all aspects of life, T'ai Chi concretizes it through moving. This implies, that change, as a life principle, can be acted upon consciously through the act of moving. The very slowness of the movements in T'ai Chi heightens the perception of minute changes of balance and imbalance.

The fundamental dynamic process of change and balance is a noticeable characteristic of the psyche, and efforts of the mind and physical effort are closely interrelated. Indeed, the one profits from the other. Movement can serve either as a proving ground of the mind, or as a conceptual source of new perceptions. This probably explains what makes T'ai Chi Chuan so attractive in today's world.

Technique

T'ai Chi Chuan is an austere movement ritual of complete formal clarity. The prescribed posture and the sequence of the movement figures are more or less unchangeable. Although movement variations are found in different styles such as Yang, Chen, Wu, or Sun, taking a decision to learn a particular style, usually means that one is going to stay with it. There is a "short" version (about ten minutes) and a long version (about 25 minutes). It can be done with a partner, in a group or alone.

In the long form of the Yang style, as Geddes taught it, each movement figure correlates with a particular breath rhythm and a particular symbol. Since moving in this way is, at first, unusual, memorizing the movement figures takes time.

The slowness of the movements promotes perception, for they evoke thoughts and feelings that originate in subtle physical processes. This implies a sharpening of self-awareness: How am I standing? How am I moving through space? How does it feel to move? What comes to mind while I am doing the moves? Since movement generates change, the thoughts and feelings of the mover undergo change as well. It is crucial that changes in postures, thoughts and feelings be registered, without clinging to them. Moving uninterruptedly is like an experience of flowing, also in terms of thought and feeling. Since, in this technique, one is concentrated and, at the same time, relaxed, moving in T'ai Chi Chuan usually stimulates a feeling of peaceful serenity. As brain research shows, these states of mind generally promote an increased resistance to stress.

The setting
T'ai Chi is best performed in a quiet environment: in a warm room without a harsh light, or out of doors in a place where one is undisturbed. One doesn't speak while moving. Silence makes it possible to hear one-

self speaking through movement. It is advantageous, but not necessary, to move someplace where one is not distracted by too many objects. Uncluttered space enhances the ability to concentrate on oneself.

Posture and movement
Posture is of central importance. Yang Chen Fu (1883 – 1936), grandchild of the founder of the Yang style and himself the founder of the Yang school in China, laid out fundamental principles of posture and movement stipulations.

Posture:
1. *Imagine that the back of the head is suspended from a silk thread and carry it straight.*
2. *Let the chest sink, and raise the upper back.*
3. *Loosen the waist, and let the pelvis fall.*
4. *Let the shoulders fall, lower the elbows and relax the wrists.*
5. *Differentiate between full and empty weight of the feet and legs.*
6. *Use your will, but do not force anything.*
7. *Coordinate the movements of the upper and lower body.*
8. *Unify internal and external movements.*
9. *Let the movements flow without interruption.*
10. *While moving focus on serenity.*

Technical stipulations:
- an upright stance and slightly bent, i.e. relaxed knees
- the distance between the feet in upright stance measures the distance between both hips
- at least the sole of one foot must remain in full contact with the floor
- when taking a step, weight must shift from the heel over the arch to the ball of the foot
- the foot only assumes the full weight of the body when the sole is in complete contact with the floor

- the arms are held slightly bent during every movement
- the eyes are opened easily and the gaze is directed forward, without focusing on a particular point in space; the direction of gaze follows the movement of the head in its relation to the movement of the torso
- the face muscles are relaxed, the mouth is closed
- the tongue lies easily in the cavity of the mouth and the tip of the tongue rests behind the upper teeth at the gums

Procedure

The succession of movement figures is performed as one slow and flowing sequence without pauses. As long as the sequence of movements is, at the beginning, unfamiliar, it will not be perceived as a whole, but as a succession of more or less unrelated segments. Although the movement figures are exact and predetermined, individual physiological needs may always be taken into account. The participants reproduce the postures and movements of the teacher as clearly as possible in order to assimilate them through practice and make them their own. The long form, Yang style is executed in about twenty minutes. It can be done at first toward the right and then toward the left, which takes twice the time. When performed by a couple, the partners begin by facing each other at a distance of about six and a half feet. One partner does the sequence toward the right, while the other, like in a mirror, moves first toward the left. Whether moving as a couple or in a group, the participants try to coordinate their movements at the same speed.

Breath

In T'ai Chi Chuan breathing guides and coordinates the movement sequence. Movements backwards are usually done with inhaling, forward movements with exhaling. Sweeping movements require slow breathing; smaller movements require short breaths.

Breathing is anchored in the brainstem and steered by the vegetative nervous system. It is an involuntary physiological act and it is easily observed. This can prove useful for concentration. Whereas, on a **physical level**, it is impossible not to breathe, the quality of breathing can be influenced in terms of speed and depth. On an **emotional level**, a modification of breathing due to relaxation, tension or concentration is easily felt. Tension provokes a tendency to hold one's breath; fear takes one's breath away. On an **intellectual level**, breath symbolizes life. This metaphor can be found in many cultures. In Christianity, Judaism and Islam, God awakened the first beings to life through breath. In ancient Greek culture "pneuma" refers to a breeze or air, and, simultaneously, to soul or spirit. Taoism relates breath to Chi, the life force. Concentrating on breathing promotes awareness of one's own physicality and usually has a positive effect on the mind, for breathing exercises are, in general, relaxing.

The quality of breathing can also be affected through imagination. Imagine, for example, that breath is not only circulating through the nose, mouth and the windpipe, but throughout all the parts of the body. When imagining "bones breathing", for example, one can visualize their various forms, cavities, and the bone marrow. Inhaling is frequently associated with energy, light, Chi, the life force, and exhaling is associated with an expulsion of impurities accrued in the body. Here, for example, one can imagine, that there are small perforations at the ends of the toes, at the base of the spine and at the fingertips, through which Chi is able to enter the body.

Through visualization, the path of the breath can be followed step by step, as it moves through all the separate parts from the lower to the upper body. This sharpened awareness can then be activated each time one starts to do T'ai Chi Chuan with "five opening breaths", i.e. five long and deep breaths, inhaling and exhaling. Visualize the body and its three central points of support simultaneously: the center of the balls of the feet referred to as the "center of the bubbling fountain"; a region the breadth of two fingers under the navel, named "Tan T'ien" and the apex of the head. Imagine, through breathing, that these centers connect with one another and breath, like a fountain, is bubbling throughout the entire body.

Water

The symbol of water appears in several places in the procedure of T'ai Chi Chuan, and always in connection with a demanding situation. (See "look for the golden needle at the bottom of the sea" or "the snake slides down into the water"). Completing this undertaking is a success that signifies progress for the person involved. Observing the essential characteristics of water and relating these to body movement refines the perception of body and mind. Pointing out the correspondence between aspects of everyday life and aspects of nature is an old Chinese tradition. While doing T'ai Chi, one imagines that, like water, the movement figures plumb the deepest cavities and then flow slowly on, like water that is flowing from the source to the brook and then onward in the river to the sea. There the water continues to circulate by evaporating, forming clouds, and returning as rain to the earth where, once again, it is harbored in a spring. And the cycle begins anew, without beginning, without ending. The flowing progression of movement figures in T'ai Chi Chuan can symbolize the same cycle, and, by so doing, consciously correlate the simultaneous physical, emotional and mental experience each time they are repeated.

Water has always taken a particular place in Chinese culture, where it has often shown itself to be an uncontrollable natural force. The Yellow River and the Jangtsekiang, both immense bodies of water, swelled and overflowed in the rainy season taking cultivated fields, houses and people with them in the floods. At the same time water is, in the rice fields, an existential necessity. A number of Chinese myths recount how the gods attempt to restore balance among the forces of nature, so that people not only survive, but that they are also capable of fully realizing their cultural potential. Water was observed very carefully in order to draw conclusions about human conduct. Such observations are described and interpreted in the three thousand year old oracular book of wisdom, the "I Ching". Water is the 29th sign, and it indicates how one is to react best in the face of danger.

Gravitation forces water to always flow to the very bottom of the deepest cavity, fill it, and, when it overflows, to move on. Its flow always seeks, without exception, the deepest places, and, through gravitation, always finds a way to move on. It cannot, without mechanical help, move upwards at all. Obstacles are able to detain it until, like a waterfall, it finds its way downward again, seemingly unconcerned by the depth of the plunge. Whether in the form of a stream, an ocean, a rivulet or a drop, water always remains itself, always retains its characteristic ability to adapt to the surroundings, and explore them fully before flowing on. It always does flow on, is never motionless, and never stays longer than necessary in order to fill the deepest cavities.

This thoroughness is fascinating. The fact, that water is the major constituent of the human body implies that, as an immanent physical trait, it also relates to the mind. The contents of the "I Ching" exemplify the interrelation of things without and within. It proposes that one acknowledges all life events earnestly, that difficulties be examined with care, that one does that, which must be done, and then, that one moves on. Nothing actually forces one to dwell, physically or mentally, on a particular problem longer than absolutely necessary. One could simply let go of it as soon as it is solved. Returning repeatedly in thought to a problem that is irritating, because it cannot yet be solved, evokes the connection between water and danger. Although water does not avoid the danger of the plunge, it does not become imprisoned by it either.

It flows on. In other words, even if danger cannot always be avoided, it is not necessary to become a prisoner of the stress that accompanies it. If, by force of habit, one dwells too long on a problematic situation, it has actually been underestimated. Observing water can be helpful in difficult situations. Take the situation seriously, live through it attentively, let go of it and move on.

Movement in T'ai Chi Chuan brings water to mind. The movement figures always direct themselves, without physical contortion, toward the deepest place. The movement sensations of the torso, the arms and the legs signal, when, in a movement figure, one has arrived there. Although certain physical mechanisms automatically regulate the resistance of movement to gravitational pull, T'ai Chi demands continual awareness of how gravity is affecting the body from one moment to the next. One never skips over the natural limitations of individual possibilities. This awareness is abetted by the slowness of the moves. The symbol of water is very helpful here.

This is about tapping ones physical and mental capacities to their full potential. This type of success is accompanied by a fulfilling feeling of contentment that results out of knowing that one has invested one's entire effort.

A historic passage from the Tao-Te-King, chapter 78, thematizes a particular characteristic of water, namely that, although it is soft, it can vanquish hardness. The above passage is said to have been formulated by Lao-tse, the celebrated philosopher and one of the founding fathers of Taoism, who lived in the fifth century B.C., and is considered to have possessed great wisdom and even magical powers. In circa 960 A.D. Ch'ao Pu-chih, a celebrated and honored artist of the Sung period, and keeper of the emperor's seal, painted a depiction of Lao-tse seated on an ox[5]. This image relates to a popularized ancient legend about the origin of the Tao-Te-King. The tale is told as follows. (See Brecht[6]):

Lao-tse, a wise, old man, felt discouraged. As scholar, he had spent all his life studying and teaching, but now that the world seemed to be heading on a downhill path of irrationality and meanness, study seemed futile. So he decided to retreat from public affairs. He was frugal, and after packing his few belongings, he mounted an ox that was being led by a young boy, and they set out calmly for the mountains. After a time they arrived at the border. When a customs official asked the old man, if he had something to declare, the boy responded negatively, saying that, since the old man had been a scholar, his most valuable possessions were his thoughts and his knowledge. This aroused the curiosity of the customs official, for it wasn't every day that he met up with a scholar. As the voyagers were preparing to start out again, he stopped them and asked if the old man had discovered anything in particular. The boy answered, "Yes, namely that the softness of water is stronger than hardness, for although it is soft and weak, water gnaws away at the cliffs." This insight intrigued the official, who wanted to know more. He invited the travelers to be his guests and, since he was interested in such words of wisdom, he asked the old man to write down his thoughts for him. One could see that despite the customs official's tiresome existence he had nonetheless kept his thirst for knowledge. How could the old man refuse? He accepted the official's invitation and dictated 81 poems to his young companion in which he set down all his insights. The boy handed these over to the customs officer, who then allowed them both to continue their journey.

In this legend, the customs official's actions correspond with the image of water. Presuming, by professional force of habit, the existence of something of value in his meeting with the old scholar, he was able to gain access to the declared spiritual valuables by asking a simple question, and making an invitation. Investing his potential for inquisitiveness, and availing himself of his own means, he received an abundance of wisdom in return, that even today, 2,500 years later, is still prompting reflection.

Softness vanquishes hardness, just like water gnaws away at stone. Chang San Feng was reminded of this wisdom in the 14th century when, after witnessing the fight of a snake and a crane, it led him to develop a form of martial art that was destined to become T'ai Chi, as it is known today. The strength behind the water's softness is the tenacity of its perpetual movement. Its effect will only become visible after a long period of time that spans many generations of human life. Since the period of time that spans one's own lifetime is comparatively short, the manifestation of this fundamental principle will not always be immediately visible. Observing natural phenomena can, however, prolong the passage of time in human perception. Certain forms of meditation also offer the possibility of extending the perception of the passage of time, and result, in some cases, in the ability to experience a feeling of eternity. Steadfast observation sharpens the ability to perceive those situations that evoke Lao-tse's insight: "Softness vanquishes hardness". T'ai Chi Chuan strives for just that. The softly sustained movements strengthen body and mind in a way that promotes the ability to find ways of resolving difficult issues.

Ch'i

All vital processes in nature are sustained and regulated by energetic procedures. This flow of energy is noticeable in a number of ways. When hungry, physical energy is channeled into movement in order to go to the refrigerator and get something to eat. Strong physical and mental energies enable multi-faceted undertakings. Illness goes hand in hand with the lack of energy. The way one perceives one's own energy household, determines well being. The shaping of life energy is a major focus of ancient Chinese thought. The ability to apply one's energy to be able to win has, until today, remained the goal of martial art. "Ch'i" is a common Chinese concept for vital energy.

Ancient Taoist philosophy recognizes three types of energy: **Ching**, material energy, **Ch'i**, vital energy, and **Shen**, mental and spiritual energy. Ch'i is evident in breathing. It originates in Ching and leads to Shen.

Ching relates to matter. It is present in the nourishment that the body metabolizes into life-giving substances. Transformed into the cells, blood or bone substance that all constitute the body, nourishment serves biological fitness enabling the maintenance of vitality and the capacity to recreate. In human beings, as well as animals the will to survive is, however, stronger than the sexual drive. Under great stress, basic survival activities such as eating, drinking and sleeping, replace the focus on sexual energy.

Ching alone does not, however, suffice as a perspective enabling the description of human nature. Two further categories enable life. As a fundamental energy resource, Ching is transformed through breathing into **Ch'i**. The close relation between Ch'i and breathing makes sense. The intake of oxygen and the expulsion of harmful carbon dioxide is a requirement of metabolism. Although breathing is involuntary it is highly influenced by the state of the psyche. Breathing in a relaxed state differs from breathing under stress. The brain registers and regulates biological processes according to the state of the psyche. Breath and the experience of vital energy are thus interrelated. Although present-day neurobiological knowledge was unavailable to the ancient Chinese, their writings contemplate nonetheless the intimate correspondence between breath and energy as Ch'i.

The transformation is furthered through breathing exercises. Ch'i is transformed into **Shen**, spiritual and mental energy, the divine energy of the gods. Indeed breathing exercises can provoke a state of mind that differs greatly from everyday consciousness. They can result in the experience of mental clarity, lucidity, clairvoyance and even enlightenment, which all leave a profound impression on the participant. Since such experiences contrast strongly with everyday perception, they were ascribed to the divine. Descriptions of deep religious experiences in our times are similar. Neurobiological research has also shown that certain breathing techniques are capable of generating unusual states of consciousness. These experiences are referred to as "oceanic" and they are, in some cases accompanied by entirely new perspectives on existence. It is not surprising that a feeling of exaltation, of being transported "above and beyond" the habitual concerns of everyday living, tends to invoke the supernatural or the divine.

A component of Shen, that is always readily accessible, is usually referred to as spirit, thought, cognition, reason, intellect, and/or imagination etc. Everyday experience shows here, as well, that it is easier to think when relaxed, and if a clear head is needed when stressed, one's own breathing pattern seems to be saying, "Take a deep breath". The ancient Chinese referred to this procedure as the transformation of Ch'i to Shen.

Spiritual capacity enables the development of helpful perspectives on shaping one's own world. Shen thus finds its way back to matter and the cycle of change can begin anew. Working in the garden offers a good example of this process. Shen is responsible for the planning of the garden, planting, its cultivation and harvesting. The way these phases evolve depends on the weather and the seasons, and it is necessary to know about this and understand it in order to harvest the plants that grow and supply nourishment for developing Ching, material energy. This process is a pleasurable experience that stimulates Ch'i. Shen can, thus, become available for the development of further garden projects.

Taoism conceives of the body as a laboratory, in which different energies constantly undergo change. Breath is always a part of the process. Certain movement and breathing exercises have a supportive effect on these changes. Their realization always places Ch'i as a link between Ching and Shen. As a component of the name, T'ai Chi Chuan, Ch'i indicates its goal. T'ai is the path. Ch'i is life energy. Chuan means 'fist' and signifies action. T'ai Chi Chuan is concerned with actively and individually forging one's own path through life by using one's own energy.

Chang San Feng[7] (1279 – 1368) offers a vivid description of the correlation between Ch'i and moving. The movements are like a string of pearls, softly threaded and flexible. No one body position is more important than another, all moves are executed with a regularity that makes the form shine quietly from within, like perfectly matched pearls that adapt themselves softly to the throat and neck of the bearer. The movements are not spectacular, but carried by an inner serenity that, from one moment to the next, permits awareness without especially emphasizing any one of the moves. The feet, the legs and the pelvis seem to move in constant unity. The pelvis leads the movement, the feet ground it, and the legs provide stabilization. This applies to all movements, be they toward the right or the left, forwards or backwards, upwards or downward. The torso, head and hands carry out the impulses initiated by the pelvis. During the succession of moves, consciousness directs itself toward dynamic balance. When turning toward the right, one pays attention to the left side of the body and vice versa. This also applies to movements upward and downward, forward and backward. When attacking, one must remain conscious of the option of retreat, in order to be able to react at the right moment. In order to facilitate centrifugal force, a slight pressure in a downward direction can be an advantage before doing a movement upward.

Chang San Feng places particular importance on the distribution of weight. He refers to "empty" and "full" weight in reference to both the feet and the whole body. Movement in T'ai Chi schools the perception of the mover to register the finest shifts of weight. Stability depends on the capacity to adapt one's movements to changes in the surface of the floor. "Empty" and "full" imply simply, that the mover is capable of testing and regulating balance. This schooling aims at healthy living.

Footsteps on the path

Feet have a significant task, for they assume the full weight of the body throughout an entire lifetime. They support its skeleton, muscles, organs, fat, blood vessels, lymph nodes and the complete nervous system. Compared to other parts of the body the achievement of these two small members is remarkable. They adapt themselves to every change of weight and/or movement in order to sustain balance. When the feet sweat or feel cold, they are "broadcasting a weather report". Painful feet cannot be ignored. (See walking shoes and blisters). The wrong shoes can thoroughly ruin a hike.

The sensory cells of the feet, joints and muscles inform the brain about the surface one is standing on, and how one is moving across the floor. The body is furnished with approximately ten million touch sensors, and many of these are located in the feet. They react sensitively to touch, stretch, pressure and vibration, all of which is particularly apparent during a foot massage. The sensory information registered by the feet is conducted to the brain in a millisecond. Certain parts of the body, like the feet, transmit more information to the brain than others, and, accordingly, these occupy more space. Since information from the feet arrives at one place in the brain, while commands relayed to the feet by the brain are formulated in another place, information concerning the feet refers to several localities in the brain. These are networked closely. Everything important concerning experiences involving the feet is stored in the brain. This phenomenon could be designated as "foot memory".

Energy zones partition the feet. Traditional Chinese medicine specifies their meridians and acupuncture points. These connect with a myriad of body functions. In foot reflexology massage certain areas of the foot are treated in order to influence the function of certain organs. Consequently, feet can be regarded as tactile organs of sense perception.

Since, with time, many of the movements of the feet become second nature, one is no longer conscious of doing them. One is, for example, usually not conscious of how one is walking, or, in many cases, that one is walking at all. Walking is simply something one does. Since memories of the first six years of childhood are more or less inaccessible, one cannot remember the process of learning to walk in the first place. One is only conscious of processes that are momentarily actualized on account of their innovation or importance.

Doing T'ai Chi one learns to walk again. The slow shifting of weight from the heel, onto the arch and then finishing on the ball of the foot schools a differentiated consciousness of momentary physical processes. This consciousness informs of momentary stance, walk, posture, as well as the thoughts, and feelings that occur in conjunction with them. These new self-experiences engender new networks in the brain that make old habits recognizable as such, and offer new habits to replace them. The advantage here lies in the slowness of the movements and heightened awareness. Enough time is available to stimulate change and stabilization.

Being "en route" or "setting out" usually implies heading toward a specific goal and wanting to proceed unerringly until it has been reached. This notion documents the way Christian thought has marked Western culture with a linear concept of time. There is a beginning and an end, and the human being is moving along a time line between these two poles. Eastern thought is marked by a cyclical concept of time, in which there is no beginning and no end. This is a salient image in T'ai Chi Chuan. According to the principle of reincarnation, existence can be repeated endlessly, as long as the repetition is sensible for the ego.

Taoism sees linear and cyclical thinking as interrelated. On the one hand, there is **Tao**, the ultimate source of all existence. This path is perceived as linear, and, after setting out, the possibility of being able to move forwards

and backwards on it soon becomes apparent, and, sometimes, even necessary. Every step experienced as a change, can motivate a change of direction.
Taoism states, that the path is the goal. In other words, the meaning of life
can be found in every step one takes, and every step signifies a change. A
change in the position of the body results in a change of perspective. Every new movement informs the brain anew about the world and how the
mover is feeling about it. There is no conscious awareness in everyday life
regarding the amount of information, which the brain actually processes in
a millisecond. This consciousness can, however, be cultivated. In T'ai Chi
Chuan the body functions as a sensitive instrument of careful attentiveness
to oneself in the world.

It requires attentiveness to one's own center while executing every step
in order not to lose oneself in the various processes of change. Mindfulness is an Eastern principle. The step itself is the goal that, on the path,
transforms itself continually. This Eastern point of departure implies that
orientation on a future goal need not mean that the present must go
unnoticed or that present-day needs must be subjugated to an ultimate
goal. On the contrary, each moment has its significance. This fosters the
heightening of intuition and awareness of one's own momentary needs,
as well as the needs of others.

As a principle, change also implies being able to let go of what has already
been perceived and being able, in each moment, to establish a fresh
perspective without losing awareness of one's own center. This is the
taoistic art of living. It can be practiced through T'ai Chi Chuan.

How the brain functions
A neurobiological model

The brain is the control center governing all vital processes of the human organism. Every millisecond thoughts, feelings, behavior, dreams and daydreams, and the functioning of the organs are simultaneously monitored and influenced by the brain. Its essential task of processing data is specified in the following, simplified model. The diagram contains three areas. At the left is a model of brain activity, as brain research views it. In the center is an example of brain activity under stressful conditions. This can be compared with the adjacent area at the right that demonstrates the way the brain functions during the execution of T'ai Chi Chuan.

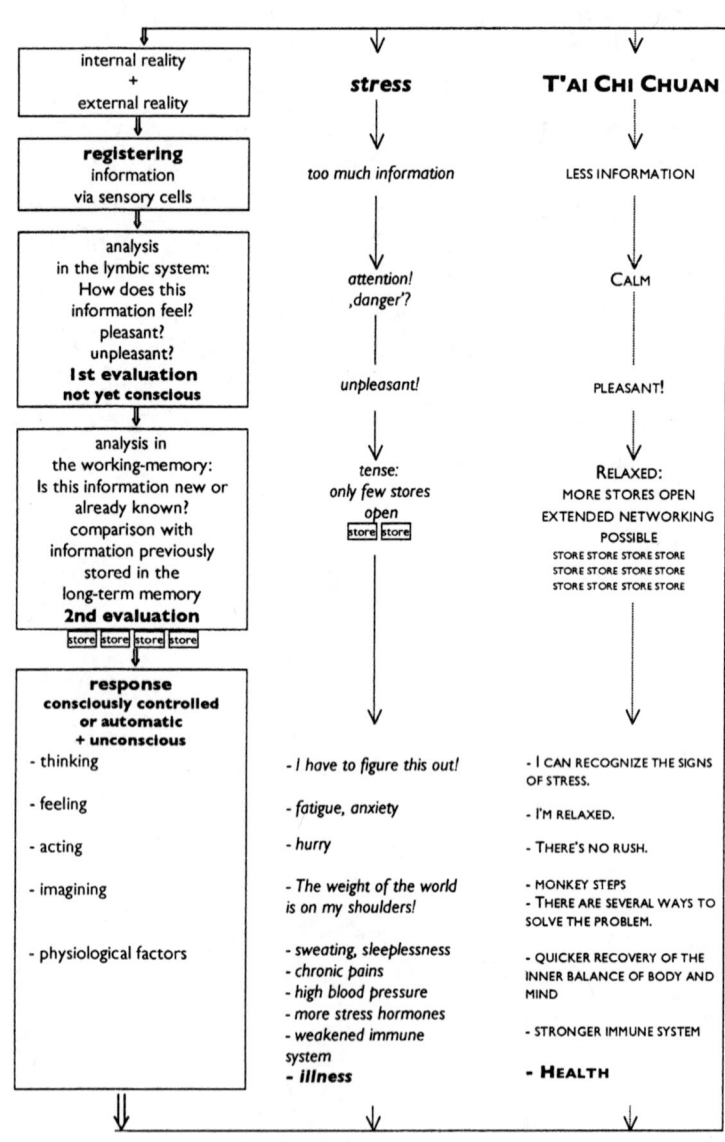

internal reality + external reality	*stress*	T'AI CHI CHUAN
registering information via sensory cells	*too much information*	LESS INFORMATION
analysis in the lymbic system: How does this information feel? pleasant? unpleasant? **1st evaluation** **not yet conscious**	*attention!* *‚danger'?* *unpleasant!*	CALM PLEASANT!
analysis in the working-memory: Is this information new or already known? comparison with information previously stored in the long-term memory **2nd evaluation** store store store store	*tense:* *only few stores* *open* store store	RELAXED: MORE STORES OPEN EXTENDED NETWORKING POSSIBLE STORE STORE STORE STORE STORE STORE STORE STORE STORE STORE STORE STORE
response **consciously controlled** **or automatic** **+ unconscious** - thinking - feeling - acting - imagining - physiological factors	*- I have to figure this out!* *- fatigue, anxiety* *- hurry* *- The weight of the world* *is on my shoulders!* *- sweating, sleeplessness* *- chronic pains* *- high blood pressure* *- more stress hormones* *- weakened immune* *system* *- illness*	- I CAN RECOGNIZE THE SIGNS OF STRESS. - I'M RELAXED. - THERE'S NO RUSH. - MONKEY STEPS - THERE ARE SEVERAL WAYS TO SOLVE THE PROBLEM. - QUICKER RECOVERY OF THE INNER BALANCE OF BODY AND MIND - STRONGER IMMUNE SYSTEM - **HEALTH**

neurobiological model

36

Every millisecond of existence one is simultaneously confronted with internal and external realities. Physical, chemical and social conditions constitute **external reality**. The human organism is physically and chemically dependent on oxygen, nourishment, climate, the environment of landscape or dwelling, and it is subject to the law of gravity. Dependence on the attention of others is at the heart of a diversified interactive network that might include family, partnership, professional relationships, other shoppers in the supermarket, as well as particular bonds with the other inhabitants of a particular city, town, neighborhood or with other members of a particular societal group.

Internal reality pertains to a particular state of the body or the mind, which is conditioned by basic physical needs such as hunger or thirst, hormonal activity, and/or energetic state, as well as personal beliefs concerning oneself, other persons and the world at large. Inner reality also includes feelings, thoughts, fantasies, dreams and the sum of knowledge that has been personally accrued.

Both realities contribute to the information confronting the brain. The sensory cells of the eyes, ears, nose and mouth, the intestines, and the organs of balance are receptors that relay information to the brain via the nervous system.

The **limbic system** makes initial, pre-conscious and emotional evaluations that are inaccessible to the conscious mind. How does the incoming information feel? Is it pleasant or unpleasant? Does it mean something good or not? If on a hot summer day, for example, the information is registered that the skin feels cool, it will probably be tagged as something **"pleasant"**. If, however, the skin feels cold on a freezing winter day, the brain might tag this information as **"unpleasant"**.

After this initial evaluation, the information that the skin feels cold is then analyzed by the working-memory. This **second evaluation** deliberates whether the information is new, or whether it relates to something **already known**. Does the brain already know about the state of the body on a hot summer day or on a cold winter day? In order to enable a comparative evaluation, the brain scans biographical information in different memory stores. Biographical knowledge implies that a major part of personal experience is stored in the brain, and can, under certain circumstances, be recalled.

An example: The brain of a 35 year old man from Gambia, who had never experienced a cold winter in Berlin, will probably judge the first cold day as "unpleasant", and then add a second evaluation tagged "unknown" and "new". The comparison with previously stored memories will conclude that no memory exists that relates to "a cold day in Berlin".

This second evaluation prompts the brain to respond to the incoming stimulus of cold. This **response** can take the form of a **thought, feeling**, an **impulse to act**, a **fantasy** or a **physiological reaction**. Response through physiological reaction might manifest itself in goose flesh or shivering. His thinking will be preoccupied with finding a strategy to solve the problem: How does one protect oneself against the cold? Who can be of help here? On an action plane, he might observe what others are doing in the cold, consult with friends, buy thick winter clothing and/ or turn up the heat in the apartment. He might fantasize that he is back in Gambia, and, remembering the hot, sunny weather get home-sick. When confronted with a **new experience**, the various responses of the brain are **conscious, controlled** and **function slowly**.

On the first cold day of the year an old Berliner will probably mumble, "It's damn cold!" get his winter coat and a warm scarf out of the closet and, afterwards, no longer pay attention to how it feels to be cold because, in his case, that is just the way things are! He is living, after all, in Berlin, and it's always the same story when winter arrives. Being accustomed to the change of seasons all his life, the response of the old man's brain to the cold is interiorized, **automatic, not** even necessarily **conscious**. He is reacting **automatically, quickly** and **precisely**.

Whereas the working-memory of the Gambian is unable to refer to a stored memory concerning "the experience of cold", the brain of the old Berliner is well acquainted with it. In other words, even though both men feel cold and it is, for both of them, unpleasant, their brains respond differently.

The **response of the brain** signifies a **new reality**. Both men have put on a coat and are no longer cold. Their brains will now, as a first judgment, register "Cold stimulus diminished", "pleasant". The working memory of the Gambian will have established a new memory store, with the content: "When cold, out on a coat". The second evaluation of the working-memory about the diminished stimulus of coldness is new for the Gambian, for he has had to put on a winter coat for the first time. Later, it will be something already known, as it is for the old Berliner. In time, **the response in thoughts, feelings, and actions** will, **through repetition**, have become **automatic**.

This cycle demonstrates (see the arrows in the diagram) how the brain processes information. **The aspects of reality that, every millisecond, are transmitted to the brain, evaluated and responded to, establish new realities.** The case of the Gambian shows how new experiences expand consciousness. In the case of the old Berliner, knowledge that has grown with time is affirmed. Every thought, feeling, action, fantasy and physiological factor is a response and relays information to the brain, which is processed exactly in the same manner and contributes to the evolution of a new reality.

Neurobiological research points out that not all memory stores can be accessed with the same ease all the time. It is imaginable that the more stores that are available, the more possibilities are offered to network information. This is the case when the organism is in a relaxed state. When it is under stress, however, the brain reacts by reducing the access to stored memories.

This is touched upon in the middle part of the diagram. An example: Two telephones ring at eleven in the morning on the desk of a clerk. A co-worker, who needs some information, is standing next to her and, at the counter, a customer is waiting, who is in a hurry because her train is leaving in ten minutes. The clerk's daughter is at home in bed with a fever and her husband is away on a business trip. She wasn't able to eat anything for breakfast because she was too busy taking care of her child, and then had to hurry off to work.

This is a stressful situation in terms of both internal and external realities. Since the clerk's brain is confronted steadily with a mass of information, its first evaluation is "very unpleasant". In such a stress situation the brain emits a so-called "alarm" that signals danger for the organism. In this state, the information is conveyed to the working-memory, which peruses stored memories for possible strategies that might be able to resolve the situation. However, as brain research shows, only a few memory stores are available under stress.

The brain's response informs the clerk that she feels confused, annoyed by the customer's impatience, and, although she is sure that she knows the answer, she cannot remember the information her colleague desperately needs. She is also haunted by the image of her feverish little daughter, her hungry stomach is rumbling, and she feels weak in the knees. Telling herself, that she has to get a grip on herself and tackle this situation, she hurries from the telephone to the counter, back to the telephone, then addresses the colleague, and, when she is finally sitting at her desk again, imagines she is carrying the weight of the world on her shoulders. If situations such as these last for too long a time, and the stressful cycle of receiving information tagged as "unpleasant" and "known", and the response, "Too much!" cannot be interrupted by a period of rest, or in the best case, resolution of the problem itself, the clerk's organism would expend cascades of stress hormones. These would weaken her immune system, and she would fall ill. The brain's response would, thus, have ultimately forced her to rest.

All those who have been exposed to a similar situation have asked themselves, how they could gain control over the vicious circle of disagreeable circumstances, influence it and bring it to a halt. In terms of the model above, the question is, how to condition internal and external realities in order that they are able to maintain good health. The answer is simple: **Relaxed realities promote healthiness.** The example of T'ai Chi Chuan, at the right of the diagram, shows how the healthful processing of information might look.

Doing T'ai Chi Chuan in a quiet setting, directing the gaze forward without strain, and moving slowly while concentrating on breathing, reduces the amount of information that the brain has to process. At first, "rest" and "pleasant" will be registered. This initial evaluation will be relayed to the working-memory, where further memory stores will offer access to a wealth of biographical memories. In this state, that which is new can be networked usefully with the old. The brain will respond through a noticeable attentiveness that promotes a feeling of well-being. The stress symptoms can now be perceived soberly, without panic. Sudden, new and unexpected insights often come about while doing T'ai Chi. The access to varied memory stores allows the brain to synthesize and convey information, that has a restorative effect on body and mind. This cycle of processing information stimulates a state of internal reality that favorizes the constructive organization of external reality.

The example of the clerk suggests, that, were she to practice T'ai Chi regularly, she would, under stress, be able to imagine, for example, the "monkey steps". She would recall the gesture of repelling that, which is negative, in order to liberate oneself to be able to absorb that, which is positive, and, coordinated with rhythmic breathing, retreat serenely with measured steps. Prompted by her ability to summon up this memory in her imagination, the brain is able to produce the information that triggers the relaxation mechanisms. This can be especially useful in stress situations, such as the one described above. Regularly practicing relaxation techniques like T'ai Chi Chuan enables the brain to formulate automatic responses that function rapidly and effectively.

Relating the symbols in T'ai Chi Chuan to their corresponding movement figures, stimulates a further area of networking, for not only movement figures and rhythmic breathing patterns become stored, but, at the same time, images and symbolized meanings as well. By simply recalling an image, like "repel monkey", the movement figure and its corresponding breathing pattern are invoked automatically. Relaxation sets in and favorizes a new reality, capable of countering stress.

The brain is the central control organ, and it is possible to school its efficiency. T'ai Chi Chuan offers a viable option here.

Change of perception through T'ai Chi Chuan
A psychological model

Turning toward T'ai Chi Chuan as a movement meditation, as it is described here, and practiced intensively, not only has an effect on the body, it also affects the way the psyche comes to grips with reality. Comparison points up similarities in different forms of meditation. The psychological model sketches the basic structure and the general course of a change of perception, which is brought about through meditation techniques. My own research (Buser-Rüther, 1997) shows, that this model is applicable both to forms of meditation or to relaxation techniques whether their origin is religious or medical.

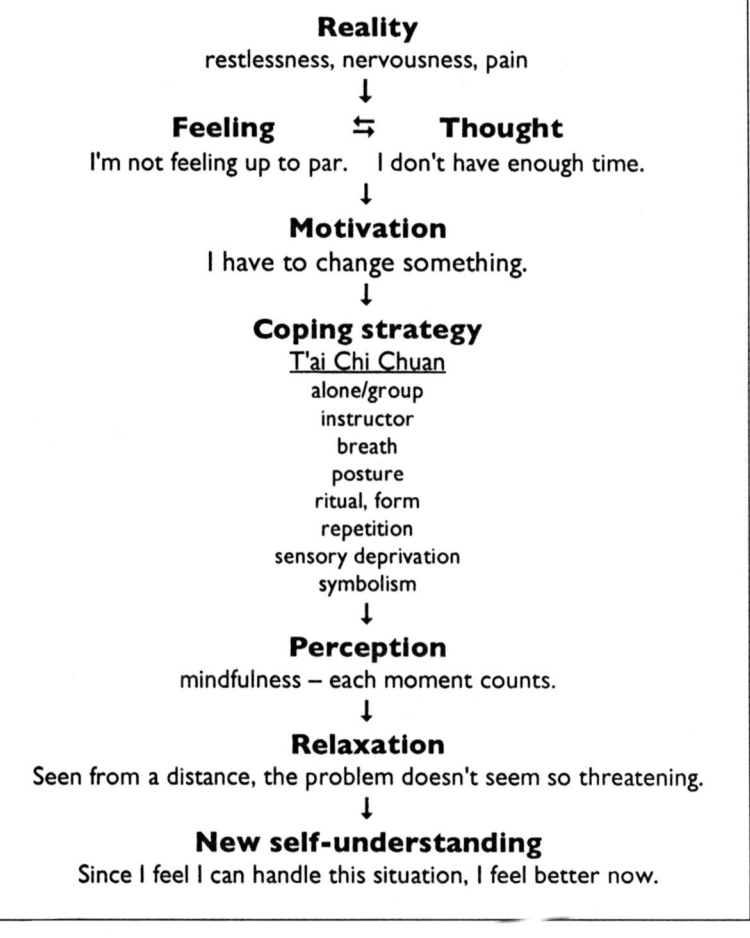

Reality
restlessness, nervousness, pain
↓
Feeling   ⇆   **Thought**
I'm not feeling up to par.   I don't have enough time.
↓
Motivation
I have to change something.
↓
Coping strategy
T'ai Chi Chuan
alone/group
instructor
breath
posture
ritual, form
repetition
sensory deprivation
symbolism
↓
Perception
mindfulness – each moment counts.
↓
Relaxation
Seen from a distance, the problem doesn't seem so threatening.
↓
New self-understanding
Since I feel I can handle this situation, I feel better now.

psychological model

The process outlined above usually begins when someone is confronted with an unpleasant reality, and longs for change. The following example is taken from the field of health care.

Reality: observable behavior and state of health

A man is suffering from frequent back pain and stress at the workplace. His family notices that he is often impatient. He has a hard time sitting still over a longer period of time and an impulse to move around constantly, to always be doing something.

Feelings and thoughts

The man is plagued by obsessive thoughts: "I don't feel well. Life is becoming more and more difficult. What should I do? I don't have enough time. Work bores me. What's the sense of it all? The children are exhausting. What if I get sick? I've got to stay healthy! What can I do?" Feelings and thoughts are closely intertwined in the brain. The feelings and thoughts of the man in question point up his loss of inner balance. Since he knows what it feels like to be healthy, he realizes that he is in poor shape, and that something has to change. He feels that he must find out how to alleviate this problematic situation.

Motivation

He considers several possibilities, and talks with his family, his friends and his doctor. Someone suggests, that he try a form of meditation, for example T'ai Chi Chuan, where both movement and relaxation are considered equally important factors of physical and mental well-being. He decides to take classes. Since this attempt is aimed at dealing with a problem, it is referred to as a "coping strategy".

Coping strategy

As a coping strategy, T'ai Chi Chuan has several characteristics that are also found in other types of meditation although with varied emphases.
  1. It can be done alone or in a group.
  2. An instructor accompanies the learning process, who is qualified therapeutically, medically, spiritually or through physical education.
  3. Breath plays a decisive part in regulating concentration.

4. Posture is considered important and is practiced.
5. Procedure is ritualized through a fixed structure.
6. The procedure is repeated over and over again.
7. Since rest and sensory deprivation are central factors, concentration is placed solely on movement and breathing.
8. The contents of individual aspects of the procedure can be verbalized with the help of images and symbols to which the participant can relate.

Neuroscientific and psychological research show that sensory deprivation and concentrating on just a few stimuli generate a state of mind, in which the psyche is experienced as being relaxed. This neuropsychic procedure has a direct effect on perception.

Perception

As in other meditation techniques that are influenced by Eastern thought, T'ai Chi Chuan subscribes to a rule of mindfulness: Since every moment is considered to be equally important, each one deserves full concentration. When a moment has passed, one abandons it in order to concentrate fully on the next. Every movement in T'ai Chi Chuan is done slowly, carefully and with complete awareness. Should a movement fail, one does not cling to it, but, passing on, concentrates instead on the next movement at hand. This principle establishes a continual movement flow. Awareness of time focuses neither on the future, nor the past, but on the immediate present. This perception process requires schooling that, through repetition, will stimulate the brain to experience change. As the ability to pay attention and concentrate fully increases, a change in the electrochemical state of the brain can be registered neurophysiologically, that affects the mind and the body.

Relaxation

Perception during T'ai Chi stimulates a certain detachment from those personal feelings and ways of thinking, that seem to have become, more or less, permanent fixtures of internal reality. These can now be experienced with a certain detachment. That which seemed obsessively important can be re-evaluated. That which was considered unhealthy, can be seen in another light. An inner calm enables the dispassionate observation of problematic situations, and softens those contours of reality that are experienced as painful. This is the response of the brain to the sensory stimuli of the meditative state, for relaxation has opened stores of memories that broaden the psyche's outlook.

New self-understanding
The man, in this example, remembers the carefree quality he knows in his children, their carefree moods, and the way their humorous comments and actions make him laugh. A realistic appraisal of his work situation results in his ability to differentiate between boring and interesting tasks and the development of useful strategies for accomplishing his work. He also realizes that his mobility has increased through practicing T'ai Chi, and that he is now walking with an upright stance. He trusts his own potential more, and his thoughts turn more to his resources, rather than his deficits. His perception of time has changed too. Through practicing careful mindfulness, his experience of time has taken on a new quality that relates to calm or serenity.

An inner meditative posture can influence the structural workings of the brain. The resulting changes offer the psyche a foundation for developing a self-understanding, that promotes well being. T'ai Chi Chuan offers a positive experience of body and mind, that is truly gripping. It is like an engram that places its imprint on body and soul.

Part 2

Symbolism

The first part focused on the fundamentals of T'ai Chi Chuan as a movement art that affects the body, mind and spirit. This part deals with its symbols. These correspond with the designated movement figures comprising the long form in Yang-Style as Gerda Geddes taught it. Thanks to her, the names of the movement figures are now also accessible as symbols rooted in ancient Chinese culture. For Geddes, the long form represented an allegorical journey through life. My own findings will elaborate on this concept.

T'ai Chi Chuan – A life cycle

The formal succession and the designations of the individual movement figures of the long form, Yang-Style, as listed below, are based on those used by Gerda Geddes. For structural reasons my numbering of the movement figures differs slightly from those she used. Since it has proved itself to be practical, while teaching T'ai Chi, to also indicate longer movements between one figure and the next as, for example, "transition" or "change of direction", my listing includes a larger number of items.

Part 1
First sequence
1. The beginning
2. Grasp the bird's tail with the left hand
3. Grasp the bird's tail with the right hand
4. Ward off
5. Pull back
6. Press forwards
7. Push
8. The bird is closing its beak, or whip

Second sequence
9. Play the lute
10. The crane or stork spreads its wings, or The crane or stork cools its wings
11. Brush the knee and take a step pushing forward
12. Play the lute
13. Brush the knee and take a step pushing forward
14. Brush the knee and take a step pushing forward
15. Brush the knee and take a step pushing forward
16. Play the lute
17. Brush the knee and take a step pushing forward
18. Pivot
19. Ward off and box
20. Push
21. Carry the tiger to the mountain

Part 2
Third sequence
22. Pull back – press forwards – push
23. Change direction
24. Fist under the elbow
    Step back and repulse the monkey
25. First monkey step
26. Second monkey step
27. Third monkey step
28. Fourth monkey step
29. Fifth monkey step
30. The magic bird spreads its wings and stands on one leg, or The bird is flying on an angle
31. Play the lute
32. The crane or stork spreads its wings, or The crane or stork cools its wings
33. Brush the knee and take a step pushing forward

34. Look for the golden needle at the bottom of the sea
35. Open the fan
36. Transition
37. Pivot – ward off and box
38. The hub and spokes of the wheel
39. Ward off – pull back – press forwards – push
40. The bird is closing its beak, or whip

Fourth sequence
41. Waving the arms like clouds: No beginning, no end (3 times)
42. The bird is closing its beak, or whip

Fifth sequence
43. Pat the horse
    Seven kicks
44. Loose kick with the right leg
45. Loose kick with the left leg – half turn
46. Full kick with the left leg
47. Brush the knee and take a step pushing forward
48. Brush the knee, box low and change direction
49. Pivot – ward off and box
50. Full kick with the right leg in preparation for: Grasp the tiger's ears and hold on
51. Twist the tiger's ear to the left
52. Twist the tiger's ear to the right
53. Full kick with the right leg
54. Grasp both the tiger's ears and twist them
55. Full kick with the left leg – whole turn
56. Full kick with the right leg
57. Pivot – ward off and box
58. Carry the tiger to the mountain

Part 3

Sixth sequence

    59.   Pull back – press forwards – push

    60.   The bird is closing its beak, or whip

Seventh sequence

Part the wild horse's mane, or Buddha steps

    61.   First step

    62.   Second step

    63.   Third step

    64.   Fourth step

    65.   Fifth step

    66.   Sixth step

    67.   Seventh step and ward off

    68.   Pull back – press forwards – push

    69.   The bird is closing its beak, or whip

Eighth sequence

The Jade Maiden is working with shuttles, or The four corners of the earth

    70.   First corner

    71.   Second corner

    72.   Third corner

    73.   Fourth corner

    74.   Pivot – ward off and box

    75.   The hub and spokes of the wheel

    76.   Ward off – pull back – press forwards – push

    77.   The bird is closing its beak, or whip

Ninth sequence

    78.   Waving the arms like clouds: No beginning, no end (3 times)

    79.   The bird is closing its beak, or whip

Tenth sequence
80. The snake slides down into the water
81. The golden rooster stands on the left leg
82. The golden rooster stands on the right leg
83. Step back and repulse the monkey (5 times)
84. The magic bird spreads its wings and stands on one leg, or The bird is flying on an angle
85. Play the lute
86. The crane or stork spreads its wings, or The crane or stork cools its wings
87. Brush the knee and take a step pushing forward
88. Look for the golden needle at the bottom of the sea
89. Open the fan
90. Transition
91. Pivot – ward off and box
92. The hub and spokes of the wheel
93. Ward off – pull back – press forwards – push
94. The bird is closing its beak, or whip

Eleventh sequence
95. Waving the arms like clouds: No beginning, no end (3 times)
96. The bird is closing its beak, or whip

Twelfth sequence
97. Pat the horse
98. Cross the hands
99. Full kick with the right leg
100. Pivot – ward off and box lower
101. The hub and spokes of the wheel
102. Ward off – pull back – press forwards – push
103. The bird is closing its beak, or whip

The contents of the movement figures are highly symbolic. Some relate directly to everyday life, either through the figures themselves or the way they associate with other figures according to the order of execution. Gerda Geddes saw the long form, Yang-Style, as a parallel of the life cycle of birth, childhood, youth, adulthood, old age, the process of dying and death itself. She also related these stages of the life cycle to other types of sequences, such as, for example, projects that begin, have an intensive work phase and a termination. Viewed from the perspective of depth psychology these analogies are stimulating. Thus begins the journey through T'ai Chi Chuan and its surprises.

Hold the circle

Pan Gu – a creation myth
How did this wonderful world ever come about?

In the beginning, before the heavens and the earth were separated, the universe was an egg, that was filled with a dark and immeasurable chaos. An enormous giant, called Pan Gu, was asleep in the egg, feeding on the murky chaos, and growing. After 18,000 years, he woke up. When he stretched, the egg shattered into a thousand pieces, and the chaos that spilled out of it found an order.

Pure and light particles floated upward and formed the sky, while impure and heavy parts sank down to form the earth. The sky and the earth had separated, but Pan Gu was afraid that they would collapse again. So he planted his feet firmly on the ground and supported the sky with his head. He kept growing too. He grew nine times larger every day, and the distance between heaven and earth grew as well. The sky became three meters higher every day, and the earth three meters deeper. This went on for another 18,000 years. By then, the earth had become very deep and firm and the sky was very high, more than 2,000 miles away. Pan Gu himself had become gigantic. He was the pillar connecting heaven and earth, for he was still afraid that, if he didn't keep them separated, they would plunge once again into chaos. But it took an eternity to keep heaven and earth in place, and when his life forces were depleted, Pan Gu collapsed and died.

Then something miraculous happened with his body. His breath was transformed into winds and clouds, his resounding voice turned into tumultuous thunder. The sun emerged from his left eye, from his right eye the moon, and his hair became the countless stars on the firmament. His arms and legs had now become the four directions that struck out from the hub of his torso. His blood became the rivers that flowed through the mountain, and his larger and smaller veins were now streets and paths. His muscles became the fertile earth of the fields, his teeth and bones supplied metal and rock, and the bone marrow provided jade and pearl. His sweat supplied the moisture for the dew and the rain. And where did all the peoples of this world come from? They are the descendants of the pests that lived on his body. That is how Pan Gu transformed dark chaos into this wonderful world we enjoy so much.[8]

An illustration from the 19th century depicts Pan Gu, the creator of the world, in a typical T'ai Chi Chuan pose.[9] In his hands the forefather of humanity is carrying the egg of the world from whence he himself had come. The egg is a composite of Yin und Yang, and Pan Gu is pictured in a posture, called "Hold the circle". The legend of Pan Gu is one of countless creation myths found in all cultures. It also connects to T'ai Chi Chuan. Certain parts of this Chinese creation myth are centuries old. In the fifth century B.C. a "world/egg" called Hun-tun (chaos), is compared with a sack, and there are allusions to the separation of heaven and earth; in the fourth century A.D. there is mention of a creator, who is born from an egg; a legend in the sixth century A.D. recounts the birth of nature and all living creatures out of the body parts of a creator.

Throughout human history people have wondered about the origins of the world, and corresponding legends have evolved in all cultures. Despite the diversity of their origins the structures of these legends are most similar. The psychologist and behavioral researcher, Norbert Bischof, interpreted this phenomenon as a reflection of the simple fact that, no matter their culture, all people pass through the same developmental phases of childhood, youth and adolescence. This applies to physical development and the maturation of the brain, as well as to the development of the psyche in terms of thoughts, feelings and acts. Bischof assumes that the myths, legends and fairy tales of all cultures document reflections on human development. Psychological research into the phenomenon of myths corroborate this assumption.[10]

A surprising parallel shows up here in the drawings of young children, which always tend to evolve in a similar way. As children's consciousness of themselves as individuals develops, circles and spheres separate the upper and lower halves of the page into two parts, and a creature, with arms growing out of its head, floats in the center of the page between them. With passing time, features gradually appear on the creature's face, hair is added in, and the legs, arms and hands are represented in a differentiated manner. As the creature becomes more and more realistic, gravity causes the body to sink from the center of the page toward the bottom.

The scribbled curves and lines of children under twenty months of age document the movements of the crayon, or pencil. From about the age of two they begin to draw stick figures superposed with lines and circles and spheres, that look as if they could be rolled like balls, or like suns. Three-year-old children draw the head and the legs in the middle of the page and, as time goes on, the figures become more and more differentiated. Four year olds divide the page into right and left halves, which are often connected by a rainbow, a bridge or a path. As five year olds become more and more preoccupied with gender as an essential aspect of their identity, they often start to separate the sky and the ground.

From a psychological point of view, the legend of Pan Gu documents the development of identity from the chaos-egg and its parallel in the scribbling of the young child under twenty months, to the gradual differentiation between up and down, right and left and the individual floating down from the center and landing with feet planted firmly on the ground. Just as the task of separating heaven and earth demanded all of Pan Gu's strength, great emotional effort is demanded of a child attempting to assume the demands of gender. The myth of Pan Gu explains the creation of the world as the effort of a human being in the act of shaping a world capable of nurturing human life, a world that is simultaneously wonderful and fruitful. Since, in their drawings, children see themselves in the center of spaces they create all by themselves, the drawings demonstrate, how children trust their own ability to create the world.

Psychology explains that the mind differentiates perceptions in terms of the categories of "figure" and "background". In other words, the mind is always on the lookout for something, a figure that stands in the foreground of the millions of pieces of information that constantly affect the senses. In self-perception, the ego is the figure that stands out against this background. One perceives oneself in the foreground of society, family, the place of work, the supermarket or the football stadium. Everyone is the principle actor in his or her own biography. This is symbolized in the gesture "Holding the circle", the "world/egg", in which the various life forces, qualified in Taoism as masculine or feminine, are constantly at play, and require control.

During the first months of life, perception probably resembles a chaotic "Hun-tun", a background of changing moods without clear contours. By the time the child is about eighteen months old, it will have recognized that it is not only physically but also psychologically separate from its parents. It can distinguish its own feelings from those of others, and is no longer susceptible, through their feelings, to emotional contamination. Now that it perceives itself as a distinct figure, an individual, the child realizes that people have different thoughts and feelings. It will, from now on, also become increasingly capable of empathizing with others, collaborating with some or distancing itself from others. The development of perspectives that enable perception to distinguish adequately between oneself and another is related to a maturation of the brain that occurs during the first six years of life.

In T'ai Chi Chuan the circle symbolizes the chaotic play of immanent life energies. Holding the circle implies the ability to accommodate these energies, and use them in order to shape one's own life. Energy is the basis of life. It should not be dissipated; it should be cultivated. In T'ai Chi Chuan the circle represents the sphere of the personal universe in which every individual moves, and acts. Perception scans this space, in order to be able to explore and use it fully. This is a challenge that actualizes archetypal dynamics of early childhood.

The first five years of life play an important part in the development of personality, and can have a decisive influence on future decisions and behavior. Brain research considers that the formation of character and personality rests fifty percent on genes, twenty five percent on the experience of the first five years and the remaining twenty five percent is determined by events that happen thereafter. Yet, due to childhood amnesia, the early experiences, which had a strongly determinant influence on what was yet to come, cannot be recalled. On account of the architecture of the brain only those experiences that are networked with the electrical field of beta-frequency and amplitude become conscious. The beta range, however, is still inactive during the first five years of life. The brains of children connect information to broader wavelengths and higher amplitudes that adults can only access during sleep or deep relaxation. The regular practice of T'ai Chi promotes the capacity for deep relaxation, favorizing the access to the energy potential inherent in the decisive experiences of early childhood. Probing the circle again and again while doing T'ai Chi Chuan can alter the meaning of early life experiences, and modify, diversify or strengthen the feelings that accompany them.

Play the lute

Why is lute playing thematized in T'ai Chi Chuan? In what way does Chinese lute music pertain to a form of movement meditation, which evolved out of a martial art? The history of Chinese lute music offers some answers to these questions.

The Chinese lute, or "Pipa", is one of the oldest musical instruments known in Chinese culture. It is fashioned from a single piece of mahogany, pear-shaped with a short neck, and it has four strings with up to 30 frets. The strings are tuned A-D-E-A, which produces a particular spectrum of chords, that sounds unusual to the ear of a Western listener. In order to play a particular tone or determine its quality, the left hand presses the frets, while the nails of the right hand pluck or strum the strings. Not only does the finger technique of both hands differ from the western methods of play, for example, the guitar, it is also requires virtuosity. The syllables "Pi" und "Pa" designate particular movements of the index finger and thumb of the right hand. For two thousand years the strings were made of silk and plucked with the fingernails. Nowadays, the Pipa has steel strings enveloped in nylon and the fingertips of the right hand are covered with plastic or tortoise shell caps. The spectacular finger technique of both hands allows for an enchanting diversity of sounds.

Pipa music, like the Chinese language and calligraphy, aims at evoking feelings and fantasies in the listener. One piece, that is centuries old, is titled "Ambush from ten sides", a tone poem inspired by a famous battle of the second century B.C. A description from the Tang Period (618 – 907 A.D.) describes the apocalyptic mood this piece evokes as follows: The heaven falls to the earth and it bursts asunder, thousands of warring horsemen gallop over the battlefield, fear and horror reign everywhere. Some titles of other works are "White Snow in a Sunny Spring", "Dragon Boat", "Dance of the Yi People", "Big Waves Washing the Sands", "Zhaojun outside the Border", "The Disarmament of King Chu". Pipa music can evoke images of nature, war, everyday occurrences, and love.

A text from the 3rd century B.C. recounts that the Pipa originated in the late Qin Period (B.C. 221 – 206) while the Great Wall was being constructed. Many people were suffering from forced labor and their anger and indignation found expression through Pipa music. Most of the traditional pieces have been handed down from the Tang Period, when music had come to play an important role in society, and nobles were expected to have mastered the Pipa. Chinese literature contains frequent references to the lute being played. It is considered a medium for expressing those feelings that cannot be fully expressed in words. The oldest poem about lute music that has survived is from 815 A.D. called, "Pipa Song" written by Bai Juyi (772 – 846 A.D.)[11]. It describes, in detail, a highly emotional situation:

The author was transferred from the capital to a small town on the Yangtse River. Taking leave of friends one autumn evening on a boat, they wished to raise a glass together, but music was missing. Then they heard lute music com-

ing from a neighboring boat that was being played in a familiar city style. The author was surprised and, seeking out the source of the music, he came upon a musician who had been quite famous in the capital, and he invited her to play for him and his friends. She agreed, and everyone felt deeply moved by her music. Since she seemed to be sad, the friends asked her to talk about herself. So she told her life story: When she was young, she had enjoyed being celebrated as an artist, but fame and beauty are transient and since her family was impoverished, she was forced to marry a merchant, who only thought of money. He was absent frequently on business trips, and left her all alone. This unwanted abandonment made her very sad. Her sadness and homesickness moved the author, who now began to speak about his own feelings of loneliness. He asked her to play once again, and promised to write a Pipa-Song-Poem for her. She sat down and began to play. The song was all sadness and heartbreak. The listeners, who were deeply touched, wept bitter tears.

Music, in Chinese culture is, on the one hand, supposed to convey emotion, and, on the other hand, to ease suffering. Consolation results from the ability to command the listeners' attention to an extent that enables them, for a moment, to forget the source of their suffering. The "I Ching" refers several times to this capacity of music to provoke a spiritual exaltation that transports the listener to a plane beyond everyday cares.

All artistic expression, be it music, visual arts, the spoken word, or movement subsists on the dynamic play of tension through sound and silence, full and empty spaces, movement and stillness. In T'ai Chi Chuan these dynamic contrasts are found in the way weight is distributed along the soles of the feet. Placing full weight on one foot does not reduce the significance of the other. It can lift in turn, place itself on the floor and assume body weight, making the next step as if a new tone is being heard.

The movement aesthetics of T'ai Chi are comparable to those in Chinese music, for, just as the titles of musical works, the names of the movement figures relate to ancient Chinese thought. The virtuosic diversity of sounds in Pipa-music is surprising. Battle scenes, for example, can be portrayed with striking effectiveness, even though fighting itself is as absent from the music itself, as it is from T'ai Chi Chuan. It can however, through both disciplines, be sensed. The sounds of Pipa music and the movements of T'ai Chi are both capable of evoking the experience of dynamic forcefulness with physical and spiritual sensitivity. The names of musical works, like the movement figures in T'ai Chi Chuan, both aim at evoking inner responses in the practitioner.

Classical Chinese music, the movement figures of T'ai Chi Chuan and the designations of them both are rooted in the world of ancient Chinese thought. It is, thus, comprehensible that the image of lute playing has found its way into the succession of images in T'ai Chi Chuan. On the one hand, Pipa music relates to T'ai Chi Chuan both historically and in terms of content. On the other hand, the formal, aesthetic character of T'ai Chi Chuan and Pipa music is also similar.[12] The movements in T'ai Chi Chuan have been compared to pearls that are strung evenly on a chain, inviting the recognition of beauty as perfectly clear proportions. Bai Juyi invokes the comparison with pearls in his poem, "Pipa-Song":

The mighty strings drum
Loud like a cloudburst,
The delicate strings strum
Like sweet nothings, a mist,
They clack, ring and echo
Like large and small pearls
Dropped into a jade bowl.

The bird

The bird is the image that occurs the most in T'ai Chi Chuan. Among the 112 prescribed movement figures it appears twenty times, under various names:
- *Grasp the bird's tail, right/left.*
- *The bird is closing its beak.*
- *The crane or stork spreads its wings, or The crane or stork cools its wings.*
- *The magic bird spreads its wings and stands on one leg, or The bird is flying on an angle.*
- *The golden rooster stands on its left/right leg.*

Ten of the thirteen sequences close with "The bird is closing its beak". The remaining three are reserved for the figure, "Carry the tiger to the mountain."

On account of its ability to fly, Chinese mythology considers the bird capable of connecting the earth and the sky, the mortal and the divine. This messenger between two worlds appears as a crane, a peacock, a pheasant, a golden rooster, and as the magic phoenix, that symbolizes happiness, beauty, dignity, long life, rebirth and a new beginning. The great white crane is presumed to carry immortals from one place to another. It also transports dead souls to the next world, which is why it is often depicted standing on coffins.

The legendary phoenix, the "red bird" relates to the southern cardinal point on the compass, and signifies the sun's fire. The myth recounts that it lived to a great age, consumed itself by burning, and, after three days, rose again from its own ashes. It was believed that the phoenix was responsible for the ancient, oracular book of wisdom, the "I Ching". Legend has it, that, as it flew across the sky, one of its beautiful feathers fell to the ground and was transformed into the "I Ching". According to popular belief, the phoenix knew of all the places, where treasure was buried.

The flight of birds has served in many cultures around the world as a projection screen for the experience of psychic phenomena that are out of the ordinary. Just as the mythical symbol of the phoenix was appropriated by shamanism, the experience of particular psychic states, such as dreaming, ecstasy or psychotic hallucinations are often associated with fantasies of flying. In these states the perception of gravity seems to be suspended, inviting the association that one is capable of greater mobility in space and time. Since experiences of this kind are categorized as supernatural, those who have them, feel stronger and more powerful than they do in everyday life. They claim to experience another dimension of existence described variously as "cosmic inter-relatedness", "immortality", or "liberation". Since the euphoria associated with this experience is engrained in memory, it tends to be sought out again and again.

The idea of flight corresponded with ecstasy in ancient China. The shaman, for example, decorated himself with feathers or carried ritual objects adorned with feathers. Trance states were induced through certain forms of dancing, through the use of animal artifacts such as a bearskin or feathers, through movement, or through crooning like a mystic animal. Trance, the magic flight, is often explained as a transformation instrumentalized by the feathers worn by the shaman, and it was compared to the journey of an immortal to the heavens. Taoistic priests were designated as "feathered wise men" or as "feathered hosts."[13]

Shamanism persists even in our times, and its corresponding psychic capabilities are acquired and cultivated through dedicated practice. The shaman is regarded as a healer, whose trance states invoke forces capable of healing the sick. Where shamanism is an integral part of a culture, people with these special abilities are seen not only as healers, but also as intermediaries between man and the gods, who move freely between heaven and the underworld. It is also believed that the shaman has a particular capacity for clairvoyance, i.e. insight into areas above and beyond everyday existence. In archaic cultures, anyone capable of entering into a trance state was considered to be someone who had mastered the laws of nature. In ancient China this competence was indeed a prerequisite for any ruler, who wished to be recognized as an authority.

Healing has always been closely associated with the miraculous, for illness can situate itself at the frontier between life and death, where the chaos of uncontrollable forces hold court. Anyone capable of exercising control here must be especially powerful. The science of religion sees this as an area of human experience where effective religious notions originate. Shamanism is also a religious phenomenon. Mircea Eliade, a celebrated researcher in the field of the science of religion, who investigated shamanism world-wide in various cultures, contends that the identification with animal figures in ancient Taoist China not only gave special powers to the shaman, they also played an important role in social and political life.

The frequent thematization of the bird within the succession of T'ai Chi movement figures suggests it to be an incorporation of a shamanistic symbol originating in Taoism. Brain research has understood how certain relaxation techniques elicit extraordinary states of consciousness and enable access to an expanded quantity of stored memories, that encourage broadened perspectives. Monastic existence and altered states of consciousness are too closely related for Taoist monks not to have known about the modified awareness invoked through rituals that integrate the movement imitation of animals. Images of animals thus found their way into the ritual of T'ai Chi Chuan, that was itself, after all, developed in monasteries.

Today, science has understood what the ancient Taoists attempted to explain as magical. We, too, like the shaman, long for control over the frontier between life and death. Nowadays medical, i.e. scientific knowledge and treatment procedures have taken the place of magical and religious explanations. Yet although scientific reality is a major characteristic of contemporary healing, the effects of age-old rituals like T'ai Chi Chuan are still accessible, and the positive effect on the psyche of contemplating mythical symbols cannot be denied. These meaningful experiences no longer claim, however, to be magical, for the critical inquisitiveness of scientific thought can explain them.

Aside from the mythical use of the bird in shamanism, bird watching was a pragmatic activity of everyday life in ancient China. Texts from the "I Ching" demonstrate how deeply the bird was embedded in Chinese thought. Although the "I Ching" was put in the service of magical thinking in order to divine, prophesize or predict, its contents are especially pragmatic and ethical. Proceeding on the basic tenet that rendering service to the community is the goal of mankind, the "I Ching" contemplates whether a particular action promotes health or harms it.

Text 62 devotes itself, in great detail, to the image of the bird. Observing birds one realizes, that, although they are able to ascend to great heights, they never surpass given limits. The common buzzard, for example, does not, of course, fly close to the sun, even though it sometimes appears that way to us below. Birds always return to the ground. Their conduct generates the insight of moderation. Their actions seem to be saying: Never venture out too far, and fulfill everyday tasks humbly and thoroughly.

Observing young birds also offers a practical tip for everyday living. Young birds only abandon the nest after their senses are functioning fully, they have enough feathers to be able to fly, and they are thus capable of assuring their own survival. Until that time, they gather their forces until they are ready to be used fully. The lesson here is, not to start something, before one is certain, that it can be finished, i.e. wait calmly, gather your forces and be prepared to use them when necessary. This can increase the chance of success.

A further observation pertains to the way birds communicate. They are able to recognize each other's call even at a distance, i.e. they do not have to see each other in order to interact vocally. The "I Ching" concludes here, that like-minded people will always find each other. People, who speak their mind and act according to how they feel, inspire sympathy in others, who are like-minded. No matter the distance between them, like-minded people will find the way to each other speedily and without unnecessary complication.

Moderation, sincerity and patience are qualities to which T'ai Chi Chuan aspires: All movements are executed calmly, in a controlled manner in order to maintain balance. The movements are not, as in a theatrical performance, directed toward an audience, but correspond sincerely to the practitioner's momentary state of being. Conscious awareness of the latter guarantees movement authenticity. The qualitative challenge of this practice has to be met with diligence and serenity.

Chuan – the fist

Box!
Push!
Press forwards!
Kick!
Ward off!
Pull back!
Step back!
Cross hands!

The movement designations cited above document the original character of T'ai Chi Chuan as a martial art. This is particularly evident in the name "Chuan", – fist. The fist can be an effective weapon. One well-placed punch can disarm an opponent entirely. Various techniques in the martial arts demonstrate how to use the fist effectively. All of them rest on the simultaneous awareness of one's own condition and body position, and the condition and body position of the opponent. A successful fighting strategy also depends on paying attention to the opponent's intentions. Not only attack, but also defense and the interplay of forward and backward moves play an essential part.

Styles of T'ai Chi Chuan differ from each other according to the degree in which each emphasizes the character of martial art. The Yang-Style, according to Gerda Geddes, has a more meditative character. The martial elements refer less to fighting as a physical art, and more to the psychic reality of the practitioner as a psycho-physiological unit. The brain processes all incoming information regarding the internal reality of the body, and the biological, material and social aspects of external reality. As mentioned previously, this processing is only partially conscious. The slow pace of the T'ai Chi Chuan ritual enables heightened perception. Since the detailed perception of modification processes, be these physical or mental, grow with increased vigilance, the internal and external principles of martial art can, for example, be observed and associated in movement.

Fighting elements demonstrate a way to exercise will power, the way thoughts and feelings contribute to a personal action, and how someone, in habitual and unusual situations, structures personal existence. Since self-control relies to a major degree on will, the fist, "Chuan", can be seen as a symbol of will power. Personal life-energy is literally taken in hand: the fingers close around it, the thumb covers it and then guides it in a desired direction. This gesture characterizes free will. T'ai Chi Chuan schools the use of will power and vital energy in order to promote life. This ability depends on accurate observation of both internal and external realities.

Instructions for fighting are direct and unequivocal in T'ai Chi Chuan. They aim at rapid and forceful action. The body parts move, without the slightest divergence, along straight paths through space. Taking direct action in this way is only possible and sensible with a clear mind, for otherwise fighting would probably resemble thrashing one's arms about wildly to no effect. This insight also relates to the way reality is being handled. When prompt and direct intervention is grounded in accurate perception and the strength of good judgment, it becomes self-evident, when action is called for, when it might be better to wait, or when it is best to let an opponent take the first step. In T'ai Chi Chuan, fighting does not aim at winning or losing; it is concerned with the dynamic realization of polar aspects of existence. Although the unequivocal gestures may look like fighting, the slow pace of the ritual makes it physically and spiritually possible, even in fighting, not only to perceive, but also to balance opposing forces.

T'ai Chi Chuan is also called "shadow boxing". This can incite the erroneous notion of fighting with something intangible or boxing to no effect, because the fight is only with a shadow in the first place. Uninformed observers might indeed find T'ai Chi Chuan puzzling. They might ask: Where is the opponent? Who is the opponent one is fighting with? The answer to that question can only be found in an understanding of T'ai Chi Chuan as a movement art rooted in Chinese tradition and philosophy. Contemporary brain research and psychology do, however, present findings that can offer an understanding of the psycho-physiological processes that play their part in the practice of T'ai Chi Chuan. Foremost among these are emotional conditions such as calm and equanimity. Both of these can be triggered through calm breathing, and by moving slowly and softly. The brain responds to these stimuli through a type of functioning that induces a potential for thinking constructively. In this particular state, the use of will power or "the use of the fist" conveys a feeling of tranquil clarity. This state of mind, as brain research has shown, strengthens the immune system. Calm and equanimity coupled with strengthening movements are fundamentals of healthful living.

The tiger

The fox and the tiger

One day a fox met a tiger on the road. When the tiger was about to pounce on the fox and eat it, the fox politely asked the tiger to refrain, and said, "Honored tiger, hold on! Although you're undoubtedly brave and strong, and people usually refer to you as 'King', you're not the only hero on earth. Maybe you won't believe this, but I am by far more dangerous than you. You don't believe me? All right, let's do the following: We'll take a walk along a country road. I'll go ahead and you stay close behind me. You'll see, as soon as people catch sight of me, they're going to be terrified and run away. If they don't, then you can eat me up without the slightest hesitation." Being simple-minded the tiger agreed to the experiment. They proceeded along the broad route, the tiger always close behind the fox. When travelers caught sight of the tiger in the distance, they immediately fled. The fox said to the tiger, "So, do you realize now, how frightened people are of me? They couldn't even see you, because you were walking behind me." This convinced the tiger, so he let the fox go. The cunning fox tricked the tiger and saved its own life by simply explaining the peoples fear of the tiger as their being afraid of him.[14]

This old fable is told in many cultures. Fables mirror human frailties in a humorous fashion, and they transmit a moral insight. Humor makes it easier to tolerate the critical reflection of oneself in the mirror of the fable, and it can encourage change. Fables evolved in times of political repression. When it was dangerous to speak one's mind, or oppose the authorities, the fable was a clever means to ease suffering by expressing a concealed criticism of the system. Animals are often the main figures and their evolution in the stories points out better ways of mastering everyday living.

At the end of the fable the tiger is duped. Despite its size and strength, the tiger is unable to realize that the sly fox is tricking it. The motto of the story is, that although brute force may be threatening, it does not equate with intelligence. The will of the fox to survive enabled it to exploit the tiger's dim-wittedness. Or, – to use an image from the previous chapter, – the fox was able to take the energy in hand, and, by guiding it elsewhere, place it in the service of its own survival.

As a ferocious predator, who attacks and devours its prey, the tiger symbolizes destruction. The ancient Chinese believed that the souls of those devoured by tigers, are not liberated, for the tiger uses them as bait. It transforms the souls into enticing apparitions, such as young maidens, or mounds of gold, and then waits in ambush to attack its next victims. That is why, in his need to kill, the tiger is able to capture so many souls. This idea alludes to those people, who exploit others for their own shameful ends. Hence the Chinese saying "They are the tiger's bait".

Nonetheless, the white tiger symbolizes the western cardinal point on the compass where one of the holy mountains, the K'un-lun, is situated. This is the western paradise, a place of immortality and the earthly home of the lord of the skies, where a tiger-like goddess keeps order and a tiger with nine human heads keeps watch over the entrance. Autumn is the season of the tiger and his element is metal. Metal is a sign of power, for knowing the art of metallurgy means that one can produce weapons and holds thus the key to ruling in his hands. In China powerful people are often portrayed riding a tiger. Since the tiger is also said to be capable of exorcising demons, it is a frequent motif of doorknockers, or of images painted on doors and walls. In dangerous times, people painted the calligraphic sign for tiger on the foreheads of children, in order to protect them from demons. On the one hand, the destructive potential of the tiger was feared; on the other hand, it was used as a charm of defense.

The danger of the tiger has become associated with extreme experience at the frontier of life and death. Consequently, the tiger was also considered to be a guide to a spiritual world, beyond the material world, that can influence people's thoughts and dreams. It is interesting that, in ancient Chinese medicine, the tiger also became associated with the lungs, with breathing, with air. Breathing is vital, and the Chinese believed that it directs the life force, Ch'i. If one succeeds in mastering the diverse tiger-like Ch'i forces within, one has nothing more to fear. People who had achieved this capacity were considered to be wise and, since they had mastered Ch'i, it was believed that they were capable of determining the moment of their own death. They could "ride the tiger".

In the long form of T'ai Chi Chuan, the image of the tiger appears several times, e.g. at the end of the first, second and third part along with the movement figure, "Carry the tiger to the mountain". In Chinese mythology the mountain stands, among other things, for pause and stillness. It refers to taking a break, an inner departure from the daily hustle and bustle, in order to refresh body, mind and spirit. Each of the three parts of the long form represents a particular developmental phase of human activity. Every task, or every project, has a beginning, an intensive period of working through something, and a fixed term that culminates and ends. This is similar to the life phases of birth, childhood and youth, adulthood and middle age, aging, dying and death. Seen as creative procedures, these life processes can each relate to one of the three parts of the long form of T'ai Chi Chuan. Pausing between the parts enables the renewal of energy in preparation for the next step. T'ai Chi Chuan teaches that expending energy with intelligence and vigilance includes being aware of the need to rest and being able to yield to it. Depleting available energy to the point of exhaustion is not only personally unreasonable; it also endangers the well being of the community.

The movement figure "Grasp, twist and hold on to the tiger's ears" asks the practitioner the following question: "Do you have your energy under control? Are you controlling the tiger within you, or is it controlling you?" The ears of big cats are extremely sensitive organs of perception. Grasping, twisting and holding on to them demands one to sharpen perception (grasp), direct energy to where it is needed (twist), and stay focused on the essential (hold on).

Toward the end of the long form, "Ride the tiger" evokes the ability to have complete control over "Ch'i". It is easy to understand here, that taming the aggressive forces of the tiger within, is a task for a whole lifetime.

Carry the tiger to the mountain

The image of mountains plays a central role in Chinese philosophy. In ancient China people believed that the earth was square, and that each corner was a compass point for each of the four cardinal directions. A mountain stood in each corner and in the middle, and, at the foot of each, an animal kept guard. The sky that arched above the mountains was fixed to great pillars that soared out of the mountaintops. A black tortoise or snake kept guard in the North. A dragon watched over the East; the phoenix resided in the South; the white tiger stood sentry in the West, and a unicorn was posted at the foot of the mountain in the center. Countless myths surround these animal figures. Each of them illustrates a particular way of thinking, feeling and acting.

The ancient Chinese turned to myths in their longing to perceive order in the chaotic forces of nature, and to find sense in their arduous existence. When confronted with extreme and difficult circumstances people hunger for meaning. Advice was sought from oracles or soothsayers, who had great knowledge of the ancient myths. The "I Ching", the book of changes, was considered the most important oracular source. It contains words of wisdom that are thousands of years old. Richard Wilhelm, a sinologist who lived and worked in China, translated it, and through its first publication in 1923 in Europe, the Western world was given access to ancient Chinese thought. It contains numerous practical instructions about handling everyday situations, which made it a popular source for everyone. Although, to the contemporary reader, some of its contents seem estranging and contradictory, the "I Ching" is still stimulating today. Some of its descriptions are capable of resonance in our times, because they touch on something of personal importance. It can prove rewarding to delve consciously into its ancient images and thoughts.

The "I Ching" also contains worthwhile suggestions concerning T'ai Chi Chuan. The taoistic principle of perpetual movement in the polar relationship between Yin and Yang is particularly applicable to T'ai Chi Chuan. The ongoing weight transference between the poles of "empty" and "full" stimulates changes in physical and mental perspectives. The designations of the individual movement figures originate, too, in thoughts, which are contained in the "I Ching".

"Carry the tiger to the mountain" ends each of the three parts of the long form. In the corresponding body position weight is evenly distributed on both feet, and the arms are crossed in front of the chest. The body rises while inhaling and, sinks while exhaling, creating a sensation of stability and calm.

Whereas the image of the tiger was discussed in the previous chapter, the meaning of the mountain is not readily apparent. The "I Ching" equates the mountain with stillness. But how does stillness relate to a movement discipline? Although this might, at first glance, seem contradictory, the immobility of stillness cannot be experienced as such without the experience of mobility, and mobility cannot be experienced as such without the experience of immobility. This dialectical process, which is depicted clearly in the "I Ching", thematizes movement and stillness as two related poles of a dynamic process.

The stillness of the mountain symbolizes stability. Despite any changes in the surroundings, the mountain establishes above and below as unchangeable dimensions. This clarity assures endurance and reliability. The "I Ching" challenges people to seek these qualities within themselves. Calm enables overview through a certain detachment during the countless daily activities that, in terms of both internal and external aspects of reality, preoccupy everyone. Just as body movement is capable of creating changes in the external reality of the environment, thoughts, feelings, dreams and fantasies can also move internal reality.

The ceaseless activity of the brain, the steering center, continues, even when the body is not moving. When subtle physical and chemical processes cause the body to pause, or, stillness pervades while sitting or lying down and not thinking at all, the organism itself is still in motion, even though its activity is imperceptible. States of relaxation can only be experienced, when movement processes become imperceptible. The health of the human organism requires that the awareness of all activity be occasionally shut down. Pauses refresh, energize and make room for new perspectives. The pleasure of making decisions freely, without pressure and the enjoyment of being active are existential conditions that evolve best out of a relaxed state.

Until now, little was known about brain function. Experience, thought and conduct were observed in order to draw conclusions about healthful living. The ancient Chinese turned to nature as a medium for reflecting on human nature. The symbol of the mountain serves as a focus of contemplation on the rewards of stillness.

A constant preoccupation with thoughts, feelings and fantasies becomes especially evident when attempting to meditate. Suppressing as many exterior stimuli as possible by minimizing furnishings and décor, soft lighting, quiet, and concentrating on breathing, one sits still, trying to relax and is literally overcome by a multitude of thoughts and images. Attempts to ward these off by counting the number of times a breath is drawn, or by trying harder to concentrate, prove futile, for the suppression of external stimuli causes brain activity to focus attention even more on internal stimuli.

Practicing meditation shows, however, that, through practice, the inability to stop thinking can be overcome. The mountain stays put, never strays. In the same way thoughts that stray can be brought back to the placidity of the "here and now", to that, which, at the present moment, is. This ability requires a bit of perseverance, a non-judgmental attitude, and practice. Gradually the impulse to think, feel and/or react is experienced with increased detachment, and feels less compelling. Serenity can encourage the consideration of perspectives that differ from one's own, and enrichment through the recognition, that life is shaped in so many different ways.

Stillness is useful, before beginning something new, before the stress of realization finds one having to correct errors. It is worth thinking quietly about a first step, before decisively embarking on the execution of a project. This also applies to speaking, for things that are said can have an unforeseeable effect on the listener. Before speaking, it is wise to think about what one is going to say, and the words that will be used when saying it. Words that are spoken consciously can have a very strong effect. Calm implements vigilance and mindfulness. This is difficult when one is associating with others who, despite having been warned, remain hectic and press on mindlessly. If this results in something unfortunate happening, one has no other choice, than to accept it. One cannot assume other people's mistakes, but one can learn from them.

Being forced to remain calm can, however, be stressful and cause unbearable tension. Sometimes jogging or taking a brisk walk or riding a bicycle can be more relaxing than stillness.

"Carrying the tiger to the mountain" at the end of each of the three parts, symbolizes calming down and stopping before starting again. The experiential quality that is strived for here is comparable to the stability of the mountain, resting firmly in place on the ground. Calm enables the detachment of oversight. From a psychological and neurological standpoint, relaxation and peace of mind favorize changes of perspective. These can be considered to be the fundament of creativity. More memory traces and memory stores open, expanding the possibilities of association. This condition is often accompanied by a feeling of contentment and freshness. Energy is replenished through calm: Carry the tiger to the mountain.

The monkey steps

Myths about monkeys and their interaction with human beings abound in China und the Orient. Frequently, monkeys seem to be faced with problems similar to those confronting human beings. They are reputed to be sly, and often symbolize a tendency of human nature toward evildoing. Sometimes they succeed in transcending this impulse by helping others selflessly.

Extreme vigilance combined with impressive movement ability is a typical characteristic of monkeys[15]. They are easily distracted, and tend to jump impulsively to and fro. Observing such vitality can be enjoyable at the zoo.

Although, from an evolutionary point of view, human beings are related to apes, despite some similar behavioral characteristics, the ability to think differentiates human beings from them. People can, for example, imagine what is going to happen on a particular day, plan a schedule, and can also postpone the immediate fulfillment of certain needs to a later time. Among the different species of apes, the chimpanzee alone has demonstrated a certain capacity for imagination, when it, for example, carries a stick when having to travel half an hour to get somewhere in particular and needs to get nuts down from the trees. Human beings have a more differentiated sense of time: although they realize that they exist in the "here and now", they can simultaneously be aware of the historical reality of all humanity from the Big Bang until the present time, and foresee the open-end of the future as well. This capacity for differentiation marks human thought and human emotion.

All sorts of thoughts, images and feelings become distracting when trying to concentrate or calm down. This is particularly evident when attempting to meditate. What is happening in the brain? It is at work in every millisecond of existence processing all information that arrives from without and within. The way that the brain processes information is noticeable in thoughts, feelings and sensations. These are not always coherent, but seem fragmented – like monkeys, that pop up unexpectedly and hop about. Eastern cultures refer here to so-called "monkey thoughts", that hop about in the brain, and make it difficult to concentrate.[16] Trying to push these away in order to keep a clear head is like practicing a sort of self-defense against one's own mind in order to be able to concentrate fully.

Five monkey steps begin the second part of the long form of T'ai Chi Chuan in Yang Style: "Step back and repulse the monkey". These are repeated in the third part. One hand pushes back disturbing impulses. The other hand opens to the sky in a gesture of receiving. This symbolizes the fact that liberating oneself from disturbing influences makes way for those forces that promote the gift of life.

Step back

A step back is taken with the same care as a step forward: the weight is transferred from the ball of the foot to the arch and then the heel. Since the coordinated movements of the arms prevent the loss of balance, one always remains centered.

In Chinese philosophy stepping back is an essential component of political strategy as well as martial art. When under attack, stepping back can, without the slightest use of force, cause the attacker to lose balance, stumble, fall and lose the upper hand.

The "I Ching" offers a sign for the theme of retreat. Text Nr. 33 "Dun", "the retreat", interrelates the mountain – calm – and the sky – the creative force. This forceful combination is thematized in the depiction of a situation in which pressing forward would be dangerous because the opponent is too strong. If one believes it possible to ultimately win, however, a measured and calculated retreat can be to one's own advantage. Personal resources are secured while keeping one's eye on the goal. By seemingly giving in to the opponent, he is fooled into believing that winning the match will be easy. His elation might cause him to become careless. The calm gained through retreat can enable one to turn the tables and achieve victory perhaps a little later, but in full possession of one's forces. The sky symbolizes the distance of a detached calm that can prevail in such a difficult process. When it is combined with the tranquility of the mountain, it results in an emotional control that is absolutely necessary for solving problems.

In T'ai Chi Chuan, the monkey steps symbolize an important way of handling those thoughts and feelings that influence a decision. One can argue here, that it is not easy to suppress so-called negative feelings such as annoyance, jealousy, disappointment or hate. How can such feelings be controlled, when they are, after all, so direct and spontaneous? It is also a finding of brain research that emotions influence consciousness without one even being aware of it. Measuring the brain waves of someone thinking shows that those unconscious regions of the brain responsible for emotion are activated first and then, approximately a second later, those regions are activated that are responsible for consciousness. In other words, feelings have decided whether a thought is positive or not, before the thought even enters consciousness.

How can these feelings and thoughts, as well as the decisions that are attached to them, be changed? If the brain is in a state that is conducive to well-being, it will favorize the information that a particular conduct does good. In this state, countless memory stores enable information to be associated in a new way. In other words, new thoughts will be conceived und other, far-sighted decisions will be made. If the brain determines that discomfort stresses the organism, fewer memory stores are open and less knowledge is available. Even if immediate reactions and decisions might be more focused on the goal, they will most probably also be more limited, for the brain will turn to those thought and behavioral patterns that have become automatic, even if these may not be the most useful. Since they are rooted in older experiences, they might not be relevant to the present stress situation. In this way thought barriers establish themselves, so-called "blackouts", which are not only extremely unpleasant, they are also disabling. The example of the counter clerk in an earlier chapter about the function of the brain describes such a stress situation, in which the clerk's real capacities are not able to take effect. Her brain registers that she is feeling extremely uncomfortable and only offers her the possibility of doing what is absolutely necessary. That, however, is not enough to achieve an adequate and beneficent mastery of her situation.

The body is able to put the brain in a state that signals well-being. Sport, eastern meditation techniques and certain postures serve well here. T'ai Chi Chuan is also a movement meditation that can activate states in the brain, that result in well-being. Slow movements reduce the perception of the amount of information arriving from the surroundings and allow for a heightened focus. Simultaneously movements that are prompted by the process of breathing enable relaxation and calm. As a result, one is able to concentrate on what is essential: being mindful of what we are doing at the moment. Bothersome "monkey thoughts" fade, the brain's memory stores open and new perspectives emerge that feel good. Brain research has now made it possible to understand what the ancient Chinese were formulating through the image of the mountain under the sky: New perspectives open when thought, feeling and action merge in the stillness of the mountain under the breadth of the sky, in order to increase the capacity for solving problems.

The monkey steps symbolize a central aspect of T'ai Chi Chuan: Self-defense does not only equate with been able to ward off and/or counter-attack, but also with being able to step back, and yield without losing balance. This applies to the world without as well as to the world within.

Look for the golden needle at the bottom of the sea

Gerda Geddes sees the "golden needle" as an inherent creative force. Since, however, one must search for it at the bottom on the sea floor, discovering it is a task reminiscent of "finding a needle in a haystack".

Many personal characteristics and abilities are not conscious right off, and can only be discovered through life-experience. A major goal in life is discovering one's purpose, and understanding the resources that are required in order to fulfill it. In Jungian psychology, the ocean, water, stands for the unconscious mind. The activity of the unconscious mind is perceptible in dreams, or when, seemingly out of nowhere, images suddenly appear in the form of fantasies, thoughts and feelings. Professionally unaccompanied preoccupation with the unconscious mind is not entirely without hazards. It can even become so alluring that it can cause one to lose contact with reality, and be sucked in by a whirlpool of limitless possibilities, and pulled down. The image: Diving down to the bottom of the sea in order to lift up one's own innermost riches has a connotation of danger. There is a great danger of becoming distracted by a multitude of seductive options. Avarice, wanting more than to recuperate a small needle, can cost one's life. The enormous contrast of dimensions between the bottom of the sea and a needle points up the necessity of intense concentration in order to discover the essential. It is helpful that the needle is made of gold and shiny. Its enormous value is so apparent, that one will have the energy to keep up the search, if one wants it badly enough.

The word "creative" automatically evokes positive values. Used in connection with a multitude of different things nowadays, it has become overused and has lost its originary force. Creativity research defines it as the ability to generate "new, original and useful" ideas or concepts.

Creative processes frequently evolve in four phases:
1. Intensive exploration of a project or problem.
2. Allowing the project/problem to rest, and relaxing.
3. The sudden idea/solution appears, seemingly out of nowhere, without warning.
4. The possibilities of realization are validated thoroughly.

Creative personalities seem to share certain character traits: They have the courage of their convictions combined with a trust in their own competency, the will and ability to gain knowledge, discipline, the endurance to pursue their own goals, they are receptive to innovation and willing to take small steps in pursuit of a goal, even if these are tedious.

People are, in and of themselves, creations. All are born new, original, and different. Since all are part of the greater community on which all others depend, society requires everyone to become useful. Those qualities that make one unique must become apparent in order to be noticed. Whatever constitutes this uniqueness becomes evident through a personal existence one wishes to create personally. This process of self-realization is also subject to the societal environment, which permits certain things and prohibits others. If the environment refuses to validate those qualities that contribute to personal uniqueness, one will feel rejected. This is so hard to bear, that it becomes especially difficult to maintain a personal vision and self-confidence. It is just as unbearable when, on account of one's uniqueness, one feels that one must prove oneself to others over and over again. The need of approval can be a cause of great unhappiness. Friederich von Schiller contemplates this theme in the narrative of his ballad, "The Diver"[17].

A king, his knights and his vassals are assembled on a high cliff overlooking the coast of southern Italy. The sea is booming and raging below. On an impulse the king puts a challenge to his knights, in order to find out how courageous they are. He tosses a golden goblet into the sea, and promises that whoever recovers it, shall keep it. Since, in the era of chivalry, a golden goblet was considered a sign of power and honor, it was very desirable indeed. Few possessed the means to be able to acquire such a costly object. Yet none of those assembled dare to accept the mortally dangerous challenge of recuperating the goblet at the bottom of the raging sea. The king repeats his challenge three times and is met each time with an embarrassed silence. Considering that bravery is a characteristic of knighthood, the shame of the knights is obvious. Suddenly a young squire steps out of the ranks, throws off his garments and plunges into the raging waters. The crowd screams in dread. All peer fearfully into the deep, praying that the young man will reappear, and, in fact, after a few moments of unbearable tension, the youth surfaces in the swirling water, joyfully holding the goblet in his hand. Then, while the crowd cheers, he makes his way up the cliff and hands the goblet to the king. Everyone is anxious to hear where the goblet was found and how the youth had managed to survive the dangerous dive. The squire's tale paints an eerie picture of the ocean depths. The gloom and atrociousness of the sea-bottom is worse than anything the inhabitants of the coastline can imagine. The listeners are gripped by his deathly fear in the face of such horror. He pleads with them never to tempt fate by risking their lives in such a way. Good fortune and God enabled him to find the goblet and escape drowning. The king is fascinated, and, wanting to hear more, begs him to plunge again into the deep, in order to be able to report more terrifying adventures. As a reward, he offers the squire a costly ring sparkling with a precious stone. When the king's beautiful daughter implores him to abandon this gruesome notion, he flings the goblet back into the sea. The king now tries to tempt the young man to dive again by making the deceitful offer of his daughter's hand in marriage. The squire watches the princess blush, then turn pale and faint and, without a second thought, plunges to his death.

In the ballad, a young person, who wants to prove his courageousness, exerts all his energy in order to retrieve the golden goblet – like the golden needle – from the bottom of the sea, and, having overcome unforeseeable dangers, holds others spellbound with the exciting and fascinating account of his experience. Avarice comes into the picture here: the others want to know more, and try to seduce the young man with the promise of a tempting reward to dive again. Despite being forewarned, he cannot feel satisfied with what he already accomplished and resist the others. He overestimates his strength, and does not return from the second dive. Psychologically the ballad accurately describes the predominant force of social environment as well as the danger of wanting to master the unconscious, without the required strength, or awareness of the hazards such a task entails.

Returning here to T'ai Chi Chuan in order to speak through its symbols: Experiencing the "monkey steps" trains the ability to deflect negative forces and be receptive for positive forces, fostering a degree of detachment, that, like the "magic bird", through oversight, enables one to recognize positive potential of a situation and, being able to feel glad about it, "play the lute". The culmination of this evolutionary process is the preparedness to "look for the golden needle".

In their books of wisdom the ancient Chinese recorded precise observations of human conduct. Always and again people have looked for answers to the following questions: "What am I supposed to do in a bad or possibly even dangerous situation? How does one handle crises? How do I feel about myself? What is the truth?" Every religion, philosophy, every kind of magic focuses on these questions, in order to help people overcome their personal limitations by finding new perspectives through different systems of thought, and rituals.

Discovering one's limitations and finding out how to deal with them, plays an integral part in the very nature of finding oneself. This is an ongoing process that lasts a lifetime, and it shows itself, always and again, in a different light. This is Tao: the path of changing perspectives, that is, simultaneously, the goal. T'ai Chi Chuan sets out on this path. Each execution of the sequence of movement figures offers an experience of who one is. "Look for the golden needle at the bottom of the sea" symbolizes the will, while moving along the path, to keep searching for one's own creative forces. When the golden needle is found and recovered, it can be used to "shape the world", to "open the fan".

An ancient Chinese tale[18]:
Once upon a time there was an old taoistic monk, who made wonderful embroideries. People came from very far to marvel at the splendid colors and forms. They used to ask him, "How do you create such beautiful works of art?" He answered, "The golden needle makes it possible. Things of such beauty require its use." The people replied, "We've got to have a golden needle! Where can we get it?" "You have to look for it yourself!" he answered.

Open the fan

The movement figure, "Open the fan" is interpreted by Gerda Geddes as a symbolization of the act of shaping the world creatively. Considering the art of making fans and their diverse and beautiful forms, this point of view is comprehensible. Silk or paper is stretched over a basic frame made of wood, bamboo, ivory or iron. Fans fabricated from feathers were also known. Artfully painted fans were often considered to be a sign of social status or literacy. Especially costly specimens were only brought out on festive occasions. Fans were much appreciated as a present brought by a guest to the emperor's court. Artists considered painting fans to be a great challenge, and their work includes landscapes, flowers, birds, and persons as well as poems or sayings.

Fans were fabricated because the climatic conditions confronting the Chinese made them necessary. People fanned themselves in the summer heat. Special fan-bearers cooled the emperor at court. The fan was an accessory of everyday life, and everyone carried one. High officials also used it as a status symbol. Alongside leaf-shaped fans with long handles, fans that folded were considered to be particularly practical and handy.

As an everyday accessory the foldable fan could also be useful as a hidden and refined weapon of self-defense. Sometimes sharpened and even poisoned points were attached to the ends of a fan. Since they were not readily visible, someone else could not be sure whether the fan was being used for cooling or whether it was destined to be used as a weapon. This uncertainty had a deterrent effect in itself. A fan was not as provocative as a sword or saber, but it was always at hand and could prove useful as a hidden weapon. The art of fighting with fans evolved over time, in which, for example, the surprising clack of a briskly opened fan was deployed skillfully in certain types of close combat. Different techniques, referred to as pulling, leading, lifting, blocking, hitting, aiming, stabbing, snapping, moving, pressing down, parting, detaining, cleaning were used as deceptive maneuvers, as well as gestures of attack and defense. Since the opened fan made it difficult for the opponent to discern the strategy of the other opponent, it found great favor in close combat.

In T'ai Chi Chuan the fan does not only serve as a designation for the movement figure, "Open the fan". Certain forms of T'ai Chi use a single fan, a fan for either hand, or fans that open in both directions. This special use of fans trains the mobility of the wrists and fingers. The swing of an opened fan offers the experience of a particular movement aesthetic. Dancing with fans, performed by men or women, has survived in China until today as a traditional art form. Some fighting elements can still be recognized, although the movements mostly emphasize the graceful handling of the fan and the serenity of the user.

"Open the fan" appears twice in the long form, Yang style, one time each in the second and third parts, and always in the same sequence with "Monkey steps, Magic bird, Play the Lute, Crane/Stork, Look for the golden needle at the bottom of the sea, Open the fan". Geddes' interpretation sees the journey of self-discovery here. This interpretation can be elaborated on psychologically. In the often difficult struggle to understand the world and oneself there is always a possibility to generate, externalize and concretize creative potential. To "Open the fan" refers to the manifestation of personal capabilities. The fighting gesture reveals an aggressive moment, an attack that lets the opponent see one's own strength, courage, and craftiness. The gesture invites a reaction, either in the form of a counter attack or a retreat. In terms of a peaceful manifestation of one's own creativity, the fan stands for everything that one's own actions seem to be saying to the surroundings, whether these be in the form of a project one is presenting, a good family meal, or a letter. Anything one produces invites the surroundings to react. It is not possible to know in advance whether the reaction will be recognition or rejection. One must, in any case, be prepared to accept either response.

As if in a combat, one gives an example of one's strength, willingness to take a risk, and one's competence.

Geddes was on the right track when she interpreted the succession of movement figures as the symbolization of a psychic process concerning the development and ultimate manifestation of competence. The ability to experiment and wrestle with internal and external resources in order to assess them, test their limitations and nurture basic trust, all play a part in the development of self-confidence. The symbolism of T'ai Chi extends from dealing with the monkeys, the heavenly heights where the magic bird reigns to the foreboding depths of the bottom of the sea. The psychological interpretation of these movement figures infers that it is neither possible to find one's own core, nor the necessary trust, to manifest creative strength in the world, i.e. to "open the fan" until one is ready to face the heights and depths of life. Thus, the movement of the fan sets a goal that can only be attained under certain conditions. In T'ai Chi the goal does not make its appearance at the end of the succession of movement figures, it turns up in the midst of the process in the second and third parts. This fact symbolizes the flowing character of existence. As in a combat, "Open the fan" unleashes a reaction that challenges one, in turn, to keep thinking and to continue to act. In this way, life generates an ongoing process that enables the development of creativity.

The wheel

One of the movement figures in T'ai Chi Chuan stands for a wheel. The fist acts as the hub, one arm is a spoke and the other arm, as the rim, circumscribes the hub in a circular movement. Breathing is synchronized with the circular movement of the rim to evoke the association that the wheel, like breathing, is moving continually.

The wheel has a particular meaning in human history. As a practical object it is connected to the development of the wagon. Discovered about five thousand years ago, it appeared in many ancient cultures all around the world.

The wheel was an objet d'art. As an historical representation, it symbolized the circular trajectory of the sun. Some peoples subscribed to the notion that the sun was traveling across the sky on a wagon. The national flag of India bears a portrayal of the wheel of Buddha. This refers to the fact, that Buddha himself set the wheel of his teachings in motion, which, since the fifth century B.C., spread first to the east and, in our times, also to the west. Within the context of Buddhism, the wheel stands for the cycle of reincarnation, to which everyone is subject, until the renunciation of all wishes culminates in the dissolution of the ego. Since, in this state, Nirvana is achieved, being born again is unnecessary. This philosophical approach equates the repeated circling of the wheel with the life cycle. The wheel of fortune documents the transience of life, in which the fulfillment of wishes is due to coincidence, a question of luck. The latter makes one realize that not everything can be controlled. On Easter, Midsummer Day or on Martinmas fiery wheels are rolled down a hill as a fertility rite. Often said to possess magical powers, the wheel was even considered capable of warding off evil spirits. And so the wheel appears as a traditional motif in embroidery, jewelry or objects of everyday life. Various cultures have endowed the wheel with different meanings.

Chapter eleven of Tao-Te-King, which is paraphrased below, thematizes the wheel in a reflection on the meaning of existence and non-existence:

There are thirty spokes around the hub that are connected to the rim. The empty spaces inbetween are no less important for the functioning of the wheel as the spokes themselves. The same is true of a drinking vessel. It is the empti-

ness inside that enables it to be filled, and to drink from it. A room, too, is only of use when it has windows and doors in the walls, and it is empty. Summing up, one could say, that whatever exists only becomes useful through the non-existence that contains it.

The wheels of ancient Chinese wagons had thirty spokes. They symbolized the thirty days of the month. Like the movement of the wheel, the passage of time is also cyclical: minutes consist of sixty seconds, hours sixty minutes, days twenty four hours, the life cycle consists of birth, death and reincarnation. The above chapter of Tao-Te-King is stating the fact, that since so many things in one's own daily life enclose an empty, i.e. non-existent space, this gives emptiness a meaning. The emptiness of a glass makes it possible to fill and drink from it. Places only become livable when they contain empty spaces that permit one to enter, move about and look out. The empty spaces between the spokes make the wheel lighter, enabling quicker transport.

Perception focuses mostly on the visible, on that which exists, whether this be the interior or exterior aspect of something. While the eye scans the contours and the predominant features of an object, the brain compares its appearance to what it already knows. The object then attains definition in the conscious mind, which is not particularly concerned with emptiness, for the contours of the so-called "figure" define the boundary between the existent and non-existent.

The ego, as well, has physical and spiritual boundaries. One exists as a physical presence, whose thoughts and feelings specify one's individuality and the individual way in which personal existence is structured. This is how the sense of existence is experienced.

Can non-existence, however, be experienced at all? How can it be structured? Is one making space available, which is empty and useful? The table is set by arranging plates, silverware, glasses and napkins, on a tablecloth and leaving appropriately empty spaces between the individual place settings. These same objects take on another sense when they are stacked in a cupboard or piled up in the sink for washing. Even though the objects themselves have a certain value, their arrangement in an empty space specifies their usefulness.

The same principle applies to human beings. Everything that is said and/ or done can make an impression. People react to what they hear and/or how it has been said. Every word, every movement can trigger something in those, with whom one is interacting. Spaces exist between people, just as pauses separate words. These empty dividers are subject to modification as situations change. One speaks quicker when one is excited, or snuggles in closer with the children on the sofa when looking at a picture book together. By structuring spaces to create form and emptiness, non-existence is given meaning.

T'ai Chi Chuan not only aims at the heightened awareness of body movement, but also at the awareness of the empty space in which the body is moving. One learns to perceive emptiness inside and outside of oneself as an unending play of forces between existence and non-existence.

Cloud arms, cloud hands –
There is no beginning, no end

Clouds, winds and rain are interrelated. Temperature change causes the flow of air to move the clouds and modify their form. Even though this explains the phenomenology of clouds according to the laws of physics, one still fantasizes about their appearance. Clouds can affect feelings and create moods. Dark clouds might intensify a depressive state; a flaming sky at sundown can be an overwhelming sight. Small, fluffy clouds might trigger thoughts of summer vacation. It is astonishing how many things one can see, when one is reclining in a deck chair or lying in the grass and observing the changing shapes of the clouds: a crocodile is chasing a rabbit, that transforms itself before one's very eyes into a mouse, then dissolves and outwits the crocodile.

In the context of T'ai Chi the continually changing appearance of the clouds mirrors the changing character of existence. Everything changes with each passing moment. Although perception interprets known forms and focuses on them, it does have limits. A table, for example, is a stable structure, but the senses cannot perceive that it is composed of countless atoms, which are in perpetual motion. Their visualization, however, requires technical instruments, which indicate that all things, large and small, in the material world are in perpetual motion.

Humankind has been acquainted with this fact for so long, that it has become common knowledge. Hence the phrase "panta rhei", ascribed to the Greek philosopher Heraclites (ca. B.C. 500), which means "Everything is in a state of flux". A similar image is found in eastern philosophy. Yin and Yang, the central symbol of Taoism, embodies the dynamic tension between basic life forces that causes them to move each other. This defines perpetual change as the primary principle of all existence.

Tao, the path, also symbolizes this mobility. While moving along the path, every step results in a change of perspective. The beginning and the end of the path that is covered are self-determined. Taking a step back, one is able to see the whole from another point of view that enables it to be seen as a part of a larger picture. Seen in this light, the point of departure and the ending are relative moments that, in the larger perspective, lose their significance.

Executing the succession of movement figures in T'ai Chi one participates in this basic principle: the body shapes a form, "the cloud arms". This gesture, that is repeated three times, symbolizes the flow of personal existence. The clouds offer a necessary orientation. One participates in a larger picture, as well as influencing it.

One is not always conscious of the fact that personal participation in everyday existence can affect the world. The individual seems miniscule in comparison with the immensity of the world at large. All the same, things that are said have an effect, move others and cause them to move. Chaos research has shown that the tiniest change somewhere in one part of the world, can cause great changes somewhere else.

When feeling out of sorts, for instance, one tends to underestimate one's own vitality. Yet the very fact that one exists documents a personal vitality that others experience. In any case, the effect of one's own existence cannot be estimated or controlled. The image of the "cloud hands" prompts the realization that, although it is perceived painfully at times, one's own finality is part of something everlasting, that cannot be grasped. This notion conceals a great potential for the enrichment of perspectives, that can be best tapped spiritually. Since one is free to think whatever one likes, nothing stands in the way here.

Kicks

The kicks are one of the principal challenges in the long form of T'ai Chi Chuan. Not only do they place demands on the body, they also reflect the way someone handles difficult situations. A digression into health psychology will be useful here in order to explain this.

Life frequently asks one to get a grip on something actively. This implies the ability to react to unforeseeable events, as well as being capable, in a commitment, of taking the initiative, and/or, under some circumstances, even be able to fight for something. The kicks evidently originate in the martial art as gestures of attack, that force the opponent to react. A kick is offensive, not defensive. An attack is useful as long as one is not over-extending oneself, and prepared to apply strength strategically and with sufficient flexibility to face and deflect the response of the adversary.

These basic features of Eastern martial arts can also be understood symbolically in relation to everyday life. Being able to enjoy experimentation is a necessity in order to be able to put ideas into action successfully. With enough confidence, a positive outcome to something one is attempting to do will be anticipated, and a failure will not prevent one from trying again. Such self-confidence requires a trust in one's own competence.

The origins of self-confidence and the anticipation of competence are interrelated. Both have been the objects of extensive psychological research. The anticipation of competence refers to the expectation, that a personal effort, i.e. **"my"** work, will result in a good achievement. Research shows that this achievement will increase when the consciousness of one's own effectiveness is coupled with the trust, that one's actions, i.e. my **"work"** is efficient. The anticipation of competence in oneself and others can increase through encouragement, such as "You can do it", or, when facing a challenge, "Look it over for a while and then try it out", and critically evaluating the achievement after the attempt is completed. Success is registered as a proof of competence. In the case of a failure it is helpful, to analyze what the problem was, think about how it can be approached differently the next time, and to believe that improvement is possible. On an objective level it is supportive to communicate, "Show that you can do it", while conveying, on an interpersonal level, "I believe in your capability". Communicating in this way, also in dialogue with oneself, can be encouraging.

What part does the anticipation of competence play in regard to motivation? It will influence the choice of situations one feels capable of handling, for if people feel incapable of dealing with situations that seem particularly demanding, they will, if possible, avoid them. Those who have a stronger anticipation of competence will, however, trust in the knowledge that they dispose of sufficient means to master critical situations actively, and, feeling prepared to meet challenges, they might even seek them out actively. Furthermore, the anticipation of competence will determine the degree of effort that is made in order to fulfill a task, and the degree of staying power when trying to meet demands. A person will give up sooner if the anticipation of competence is weak. Strong anticipation of competence stimulates will power and healthful behavior.

Anticipation of competence can be evaluated personally with the help of the following statements[19]. Do they apply to you?

1. *I'm not preoccupied with difficulties, and usually find any number of ways to overcome obstacles.*
2. *I usually succeed at what I set out to do.*
3. *I can handle unexpected situations well.*
4. *I know my capabilities and can count on them.*
5. *I enjoy working toward goals I set for myself.*

If the above sentences do apply to you, then your anticipation of competence is high. You tend to meet both everyday and unusual challenges with an open mind, and, since the effect of a failure does not discourage you particularly, you feel prepared to try again. Should a first approach fail, you feel yourself capable of developing and trying out a new one.

If the above sentences do not seem to apply to you, you might have serious doubts about your personal capabilities. This means that you will have to work on your attitude, in order to gain sufficient self-confidence.

New experiences influence personal attitudes. Exposing oneself to new situations in order to evaluate them requires a certain amount of audacity. It does become immediately noticeable whether one feels comfortable with them or not. What is going on in the situation itself, and what is going on inside oneself are two levels of a happening that are easily observed. It is also important to realize that these levels are separate, i.e. one is not always personally responsible that something has failed. Unfavorable circumstances themselves are often to blame. Trying to influence and change them offers a chance to experience personal strengths. This encourages the anticipation of competence and self-confidence. Having been able to change something means, that the success has been due to one's own efforts. This is the necessary prerequisite of self-reliance and self-confidence. It is, however, also essential here to judge intermediary goals realistically.

The anticipation of competence does not refer to an objective estimation of someone's resources for taking action, but rather to the subjective estimation of one's own coping strategies. A slight overestimation of personal competence will have a positive effect on the outcome of an undertaking. People with a stronger anticipation of competence tend to believe in their own capabilities and they will register a success as the result of their own talents. To their minds, external circumstances cause failure. For those who have a weaker anticipation of competence, the opposite is true. They minimize personal success by finding the task too easy, for little or no effort was necessary. When confronted with failure, they feel guilty that they were unable to succeed in the first place. Self-deprecating ways of thinking often lead to depressive states and the feeling that one is losing self-control. The healthy psyche is grounded in a positive self-image. The latter requires that one consider oneself worthy enough to succeed, and the ability to experience failure as a relative matter.

The ways of thinking described above are the acquired results of life experience. Not only positive, but also negative thought patterns are part of this acquired repertoire. Overcoming negative attitudes in order to maintain the health of the psyche requires changing perspectives. Since thought patterns are usually a question of habit, they are, however, not easily changed. But change is, indeed, possible, and the psychology of learning shows how it can be done. Exposing oneself to a variety of situations, trying them out and evaluating the experience afterwards are important stations in a learning process that offers an insight into one's real capabilities. Research in this area shows that challenges that are difficult to meet offer a reliable impression of how personal capabilities are developing. Tasks that are fulfilled easily do not offer new insights. On the contrary, they leave the impression that nothing has changed anyway. Experience shows that the anticipation of competence increases while striving to achieve something. Positive experiences become anchored in self-image, gradually strengthen the anticipation of competence and bring it to the level required to maintain the health of the psyche.

Health psychological research findings show that the anticipation of competence is influenced by:

1. direct experience (participation): imitating someone else's example.
2. indirect experience (observation): observing an example, relating to it emotionally and thinking about it.
3. symbolic experience: seeking affirmation from others: "You can do it!"
4. a moderate level of emotional excitement: People with a strong anticipation of competence take new challenges in stride, no matter their factual competence.
5. Lack of experience is often the cause of failure and a weak anticipation of competence.
6. People with a strong anticipation of competence are usually able to learn how to avoid risks, and maintain health-promoting habits over longer periods of time when they feel determined that it is necessary.

How do these health psychological findings relate to T'ai Chi Chuan? The sequence of kicks is a challenge. It requires forceful movements of the foot, arm and hand while standing on one leg, i.e. without losing balance. This is not going to succeed immediately. One has to have the patience in order to find out how the center of the body must counterbalance the energetic movements of the limbs. The latter presupposes precise physical awareness, which is, nowadays, not something usually found in the high speed of everyday life. Movements and actions have, perhaps, become more or less automatic reactions. People are overly stimulated and usually feel compelled to make quick decisions. There doesn't seem to be enough time available to register what they really feel about the stimuli and the decisions, and whether they really want what they are getting. In other words, what is overwhelming has less to do with one-self, and more to do with the circumstances of being forced to decide without having enough time to have thought about the situation, and analyzed it beforehand.

T'ai Chi can bring about an improvement here. The slow procedure of the ritual not only schools physical awareness; it also increases the awareness of personal thought patterns. Not being able to master the kicks immediately might lead to utter frustration, and the thought, "I will never be able to learn that!" Or, "This is new, and I'm still inexperienced. Firstly, I've got to figure out, how to maintain my balance. But since I'm practicing a lot, I'm sure I'll get it in time!" Perhaps one's thoughts will turn to either of the two alternatives above, depending on how one is feeling just at that moment.

Any ritual is an opportunity for positive learning, and gaining self-confidence. Since a ritual always proceeds in the same way, it enables re-peated experimentation. No decisions have to be made to practice this or that element. The ritual is an ideal framework for learning. Training and learning help make an unconscious and automatic habit of those repeated procedures on which one so depends. Having to be conscious, in daily life, of everything one is doing every minute would be over-whelming. The sequence of kicks offers an opportunity to strengthen the anticipation of competence and stabilize self-confidence by learning to deal with a difficult situation, and handle failure sensibly. Taking small steps slowly, and evaluating them quietly in order to progress, also trains endurance. Practicing with others offers a chance to observe them, emulate their good examples and receive affirmation, "You can do it!" The degree of difficulty is relatively high here, i.e. practice will not lead to immediate success. Progress will only become evident after a while. But the experience of perseverance, learning to achieve something all by oneself, enables the realization that the increase of competence is due to oneself. And that strengthens self-confidence.

Slowness and softly flowing breathing induce a state of relaxation and serenity. As the movement figures of T'ai Chi have become internalized this state of mind can be evoked in other situations of daily life. This offers the experience of personal competence in shaping existence. Putting this in the language of T'ai Chi Chuan: I am in balance and can execute the kicks, i.e. my actions calmly and efficiently.

Part the mane of the wild horse

The horse has various connotations in Chinese culture. In ancient times, wild horses had first to be tamed, in order to be able to domesticate them and use them for work. They were great assets as beasts of burden or draught animals. For nomads their value as mounts was inestimable. They were a factor of political power as chargers. Tribes or peoples that had a multitude of mounted warriors were feared.

Rapidity coupled with enormous strength is a major characteristic of wild horses. Taming them requires great empathy, courage, perseverance and agility. Being able to gain control over the vehemence of a wild horse is still considered to be a great art.

Myths and fairy tales often attribute special forces to horses. They transport the gods at breakneck speed from one place to another. Sometimes horses are speaking and perform magic. They are endowed with destructive forces, and can even tear a tiger to bits with their teeth. These characteristics are offset by the image of the gentle mare, which is capable of neutralizing the aggressivity of her wild partner. In contrast with Western myths, in which the hero slays a dragon, in order to liberate a country from the destructive force of a monster, Eastern myths do not usually culminate in the elimination of brute force. They portray, instead, in a play of opposing forces, the attempt to keep what is destructive under control. Brute force is considered to be no less natural a quality as protectiveness, caring, soothing, or consoling. Dealing attentively with both opposites is a prerequisite of creative processes.

As an *objet d'art*, the horse enjoyed great popularity in ancient China.[20] Like the tiger, it was used as a protective charm to ward off demons, for example, as a guardian of graves. Burial objects made of clay, bronze, ceramic or jade also depict the horse. It was believed that utensils and tomb sculptures could be of use to the dead in the hereafter.

In T'ai Chi Chuan one is asked to "part the mane of the wild horse." One is also asked twice to "pat the horse." Evidently, these requests proceed on the notion that one possesses the qualities of someone capable of taming wild horses. This might be surprising, for not everyone has something to do with horses, and not only a few might find these large animals frightening. Ancient Eastern thought proceeds from the notion that people are inherently capable of assuming characteristics necessary to survive, and serve not only themselves, but the community and the cosmos as well. This notion is based on a particular understanding of the individual and the world. It does not, as does the contemporary Western world in our times, rest on the assumption of individual autonomy, but on a notion of universal balance: The individual is to strive throughout life, to be able to see the whole picture, and, by becoming acquainted with the characteristics of others, empathize with them, in a striving that all co-exist amicably in the world-at-large.

The ancient Chinese were not only exposed to the forces of nature, they were confronted, too, with the fury of invading hordes and the willfulness of power-hungry rulers. It is no wonder that philosophies, myths and fairy tales developed, which offered people thoughts and images as internalized support while trying to master the dangers of everyday life. The wild horse stands for unbridled force, that can, when untamed and provoked, cause destruction.

Various aspects of this force are present in everyday life: in the angry child throwing a tantrum, the enraged teenager, the exasperated boss harassing his employees, the speeding driver, or the firm that, in order to increase profits, is letting thousands of employees go. Feelings can resemble those of a wild horse, when one turns green with envy or feels blind hate. Although one usually does not admit to such feelings, they can nonetheless eat one up inside because one cannot stop thinking about them. These inner or outer wild situations cannot be ignored, for they are threatening and impel people to react.

Repeating the figure "Part the mane of the wild horse" seven times is an advice about how to approach these explosive situations adequately: Slowly, breathing calmly, insistent, always and again daring to start anew, and being relaxed, for one's own relaxed state can be picked up by the other person. Repetition and slowness result in care, and the chance to carefully observe all facets of the movement being made. Slow movements make this immediately apparent when one is not really relaxed.

The same is true when communicating with others. Not only their words and stated facts are heard, but their feelings too. Remaining receptive and trying not to suppress feelings, makes it possible to experience what others are going through inside themselves. Brain research shows that feelings determine personal actions much more than one would care to imagine. Detachment and calm offer a possibility for the memory stores to propose solutions for problems. More memory stores are available to the brain in a relaxed state, than under stress.

Meeting with someone overly tense is not easy. When feeling relaxed, one is more disposed to "taming". One can grasp the negative feelings of the other person, and empathize, without having to feel the same way oneself. Calm detachment permits a cautious approach to this difficult situation, and can encourage the other person to release tension. Getting along with each other is easier, for relaxation offers both an access to more memory stores, and the chance to find solutions more easily.

Certain situations do require confrontation, fighting and warding off. In other situations, however, aggressive strategies exacerbate the problem at hand rather than solving it. In such situations the abilities of the tamer of wild horses is required. T'ai Chi Chuan proceeds from the idea that these abilities are inherent in every practitioner und need only to be activated.

The Jade Maiden is working with shuttles
or
The four corners of the earth

The image of the heavenly daughter of the Jade Emperor, "the Jade Maiden" or "the Weaving Maiden" appears in the third part of the long form, Yang style. It is an image of someone working, and this is not typical of the symbolic designations of the movement figures in the long form. Until this point, the symbolic designations refer to animals or fighting gestures. The Jade Maiden is the only image of a human figure that appears in T'ai Chi Chuan. Consequently, it has a special significance. The reasons are cultural, and they can be approached in two myths about stars.

Myth 1: The spinning woman and the cowherd[21]

A poor cowherd had been looking after a peasant's cow year in and year out. It grew and flourished, and its shiny golden coat made the impression that it must be a very special cow indeed. And, in fact, on the seventh day of the seventh month of the year the cow began to talk with the cowherd. It persuaded him to fly on its back to the heavenly kingdom of the Jade Emperor. Just at this moment, his nine daughters were bathing in a beautiful lake in magnificent surroundings. The seventh, an especially beautiful maiden, who was responsible for spinning, weaving and sewing both in the heavens as on earth, was to become his wife. Following the cow's suggestion, he stole her clothes. With the help of the cow and a talking willow tree, he finally persuaded her to marry him, after which he gave her back her clothes. She followed him, they became a couple and the cowherd, thus, became immortal.

After seven days, however, the young woman took leave of her husband because she had to see to her weaving. She had already lost so much time, and was afraid her father would punish her. She set out and the cowherd ran after her. She removed a hairpin and drew a line right across the sky. This line became the Silver River, the Milky Way.

For thousands of years, both lovers stand on its banks night after night, waiting for each other. On the seventh day of the seventh month of each year they are allowed to meet. All the crows on earth fly up to the Milky Way, perch close to one another and form a bridge for the cowherd and the Jade Maiden. On this day not a single crow can be seen on earth and, in the evening, there is a gentle rain. People say, the raindrops are their tears, for after this one joyful night, they have to part with each other again for another year. This is the day of the Rain Festival.

In ancient China, jade was a symbol of immortality that, through the relationship between father and daughter (Jade Emperor – Jade Maiden/ weaver), gave great significance to the practical task of making clothes.

Tending to cattle was also so significant, that, through marriage, the cowherd became immortal. The myth emphasizes the fact, that clothing and food are practical necessities. Ancient Eastern societies were particularly aware of this fact, as the countless variations of this legend throughout Eastern countries well prove. Both of the main figures in the myth are eternalized in the starry sky. The star of the Jade Maiden is Vega in the constellation Lyra, and the star of the cowherd is Atair in the constellation Aquila. The Milky Way separates these two constellations. During many nights of the year they are observable in the Northern Hemisphere. Since, in ancient times, the sky was not polluted with artificial light, the constellations, being distinctly visible, were greatly admired and stimulated the imagination. It is, thus, not surprising that these two constellations were to become endowed with such vital meanings.

The myth codifies several notions. It is anchored in the archetypical principle of the encounter of the masculine and the feminine. They come together now and then and, according to Eastern thought, suffer because of their fundamental separateness. Just like the heavenly Jade Maiden and the human cowherd, they are foreign to each other. Only the guile of the cow, that connects heaven and earth, is capable of joining man and woman. Through their union the man, a human, does become immortal, but must conform forthwith to the laws of heaven, and can only see his wife once a year. The heavenly wife can love her husband, but, aside from their one annual meeting, she must assume responsibility for overseeing the cultural activities of women – spinning, weaving and sewing.

Clothing was a major pillar of culture, and symbolized a society's richness. Its fabrication was, in almost all cultures, in the hands of women, young and old, and it was laborious. After completing the agricultural labors during the spring, summer and autumn seasons, the period of homemaking began. Marriages were made, and the wives began to spin and weave in order to make clothes for their husbands and children. There was no time for love, only daily toil until late at night. The long winter days thus felt twice as long.

Nonetheless the old tales document the high esteem in which this work was held. The instructress, the Jade Maiden, was heaven-sent, and the art of spinning, weaving and sewing that she brought with her, was a service of the gods to mankind.

Do the contents of this myth find an echo in a contemporary outlook on life? The difference of the sexes and their longing for each other still holds true. Women are, of course, no longer compelled to fabricate clothing today, but the challenge of coordinating profession, parenting, and partnership is demanding and tiring. Partnership is often short-changed. This reality resembles the situation in ancient China.

The cultural difference in understanding has more to do with the fact that, in ancient cultures, daily work here on earth related to heaven, to a higher law, that absolved the individual of a certain responsibility. One followed the dictate of the gods, suffered and bore the strain of manual labor.

Such notions of higher law have become questionable nowadays, when individuals themselves are considered to be responsible for their acts. This does, however, cause a tendency to overlook today's greater dependency on overriding global structures and circumstances. Raising healthy children and successfully earning a living are not only a question of individual will and capacities. These issues also depend on societal conditions. And these are far more difficult to influence than the question, as to whether or not one should help the kids solve a mathematical problem or let them figure it out for themselves. It is mostly the individual itself, who is considered to be the cause of failure, not the circumstances in which the unfortunate failure occurred. Psychology refers to this phenomenon as a "fundamentally mistaken attribution", in which the reasons for something that happens are always sought in the individual. It is easier, of course, to focus on one individual than to analyze complex circumstances. Since human perception is biologically constructed in this way, this erroneous conclusion is widespread. Perception can, however, be trained to be able to grasp complex relationships and judge them accordingly. But the fact that human limitations are understandable does not eliminate them.

Myths absorb human limitations and invent a world, in which gods place demands on humans and oversee their fulfillment. People need only follow. But even the gods are subject to laws, obligations and compulsions. In the mirror of their destiny, people can, in part, recognize themselves. The mythic world of the gods enables people to distance themselves from reality. This attitude makes reality more bearable. That the gods suffer the same fate as people do, adds a new dimension to personal suffering. It seems smaller.

The fact, that the myth of the "Jade Maiden" designates a movement figure in T'ai Chi Chuan shows how deeply this meditative sport is anchored in ancient Chinese thought. Executing the figure, "The Jade Maiden is working with shuttles" is like entering into a particular dynamic crossfire in which one touches on the four corners of one's own personal horizon. After referring to each of the directions, one always returns to the center and holds the circle, contemplating who one is, before moving out toward the furthest point of the next direction. The goal, during this demanding movement challenge, is to remain in balance. This figure connects all the cardinal directions, all four corners of the earth. This associates with the bridge of crows, which enables the meeting between the masculine and the feminine. The movement figure also invites the association with the shuttles, which continually connect the threads from below with those above, from the right to the left and back again.

Looking up at the midnight sky on the seventh day of the seventh month, one can see the Summer Triangle composed of Vega in Lyra, Atair in Aquila and Deneb in Cygnus. Vega is the weaver and Atair, the cowherd. The Milky Way separates their constellations. These visible and tangible constellations of stars in the night sky are the material constituents for stories that human beings have developed in order to record the experience of their psychic reality – the separation of the sexes, the power of the systems of a higher order, of love and deep longing.

Myth 2: The punished, lazy spinning maiden[22]

This myth about the stars relates directly to the stellar constellations, Lyra – the weaver, and Aquila – the cowherd. It is told, that the favorite daughter of the Emperor of Heaven always sat at the Heavenly River busily spinning the finest threads and weaving the most precious cloth. It was her greatest wish to bring her art to the people on earth. This wish was to be fulfilled, for a famous explorer was trying to plot the course of the Yangtse River. While following the river to its source, he came across the Heavenly River. He wanted to explore it as well, in order to find its source. Traveling the river was especially dangerous and required audacity and endurance. He finally came across the heavenly weaver. She waved and gave him her distaff with the request that it be given to the women of the city of Canton, so that they could learn to make the most beautiful tissues. Thus it came to pass, that even until this very day, the city of Canton is celebrated for the art of weaving and embroidery.

Although the Emperor of Heaven was glad about the diligence and ability of his daughter, it also displeased him that she no longer allowed herself any leisure, and entirely neglected her looks. He sought out the spirit of a star, the cowherd, who lived on the other side of the Heavenly River and married him to his daughter. The couple moved into the palace of the star spirit, lived there happily, and was so contented, that the young woman completely forgot to work on her distaff and her loom. The Emperor of Heaven was so annoyed, that he brought his daughter back and banished her to the Heavenly River, where she was to pick up her work again. Her father allowed the unhappy man and wife an annual meeting, namely on the seventh day of the seventh month. Then he beckoned all the magpies on earth to come and commanded them to build a bridge over the Heavenly River, so that his daughter could cross and spend a night of happiness with her husband.

Until this very day, on the seventh day of the seventh month, not a magpie can be heard anywhere, for they are all following the call of the Emperor of Heaven.

In this myth, the domineering father has the right to decide the fate of his daughter. Once again, the art of fabricating clothing is at the center of the tale. And it is just as important to the Emperor of Heaven as it is to his daughter. It is also interesting that the man's desire to explore is necessary in order to bring the craft of textiles to women. The roles of the genders are clearly defined here.

It is, at this point, worth giving a thought to the psychological difference between **mythological thinking**, with its testimonies that are thousands of years old, and **enlightened thinking**, that has been in use for two hundred years. Both ways of thinking aim at creating order and oversight in a world experienced as chaotic. Each way of thinking pursues the particular logic of its own worldview. T'ai Chi Chuan attempts to merge both ways of thinking. Mythological images are understood to be a projection of inner images that formulate the conditions and dynamics of the psyche. Today, enlightened thinking enables the critical observation, description, explanation and modification of reality.

The following comparison illustrates these different points of view.

mythological thinking	enlightened thinking
Ruler of Heaven Heavenly Emperor	*Nature*
The Ruler of Heaven has power: determines the fate of the gods, people, animals and plants.	*The cosmos is subject to natural law.*
woman man	*Difference of the <u>sexes</u> is predetermined.*
Social roles are predetermined. woman: weaving, spinning man: guarding the herd	*Social roles of <u>gender</u> originate in changeable norms.*
Reality can hardly be influenced at all.	*The individual is able to act and, through insight, develop coping strategies, that influence reality.*
Human beings are dependent.	*Human beings are independent.*

ways of thinking

The snake and the golden rooster

In the tenth sequence of the third part of the long form, the snake slides down and glides into the water. It descends into the depths, emerges and transforms itself into a golden rooster. The corresponding movement figure is one of the most demanding in T'ai Chi Chuan. It requires careful legwork and a fine sense of balance. The process of transformation of a snake into a bird has a central significance: in ancient cultures it was a symbol of a chemical process of transformation, which had, however, a spiritual background. The image is known in alchemy, a pre-scientific discipline. Alchemists existed in all of the larger cultures, especially in the Middle Ages in Europe, and, before the Christian era, in China. They wanted to discover the essence of life. The alchemists believed that, were they to discover it, they would then be able to make gold, i.e. the most precious substance, known to the ancient world. Being able to produce it seemed to them to be the most important discovery imaginable. Gold is also thematized in T'ai Chi Chuan in the image of the golden rooster.

Alchemy was also concerned with finding the "philosopher's stone" or primary matter, for the alchemists believed that the divine, the essential principle of all life, is imprisoned in matter. They wished, through experimentation, to liberate the divine from matter. To the alchemist's mind, experimentation was a process of salvation. In other words, through alchemy, man was attempting the salvation of god. This vision was revolutionary, for it is the common belief since the inception of Christianity that God is to save Humanity from its imperfection. This belief is ritualized in the Catholic mass through a process of transformation in which God, through Jesus, becomes a man, who, like a human being, suffers and dies. In this transformation ritual of every mass, bread becomes the body and wine the blood of Christ. This is called transsubstantiation. Believing that the transformation of matter goes hand in hand with spiritual notions persists even today, for the bonding of spirit and matter is a deeply human need.

Although the alchemist understood himself to be a servant of god, he also had confidence in his own ability to set the process of transformation in motion. This attitude documents a European tendency to separate itself from the official church, which only awarded theologians, – and certainly not experimental alchemists, – the right to mediate between Man and God. The critical questioning of established theological precepts began in alchemy. When, later, experimentation became the fundament of research in natural science, the conflict between the church and science relating to the question "What is the truth?" began to take its course.

The practical work of the alchemists required them to merge or bond different materials in order to cause a chemical reaction, i.e. to transform matter. Experiments took place using every possible substance. The various materials were heated in a retort, the four elements earth, fire, water and air were brought into the process and the discovery of a sort of "whole" was eagerly awaited. The alchemists believed that this procedure would lead them to solve the primary question of the advent of life. There were countless prescriptions and descriptions of utensils and procedures. The most refined laboratories were to become the forerunners of those laboratories used today in the field of chemistry.

In complete contradiction to the team play of contemporary science, the alchemists were mavericks, who seldom referred with one another. True alchemy was not considered a business, but a sacred, holy undertaking, a quiet occupation, full of sacrifice. Knowledge could only be transmitted to those, who had proved themselves worthy of it. Good alchemists distinguished themselves through intelligence, diligence, care, honesty and a striving for spiritual insights. Since their motivation corresponded with the goal of salvation, they turned to meditation, fasting, prayer and the help of the Holy Spirit. Their undertaking required absolute dedication.

Beyond working with matter, the alchemists found the way to themselves as human beings. Current research shows that fasting and meditation can cause extraordinary states of consciousness that convey an experience of clairvoyance and enlightenment. It is probable that the alchemists made a connection between such an experience and a substance they were working on at that moment. They projected the transformational experience of their own psyche onto matter. Although none did succeed in making gold, they experienced their quest as a profound self-transformation.

Two types of alchemy existed in ancient China. The first, an external form, "wai tan", aimed, like its European counterpart, at making gold. The second, an internal alchemy – "nei tan" – focused on prolonging life. It conceived the body as a laboratory in which transformational processes occur. Life could be prolonged through a special diet, minerals, herbs, a particular breathing technique and certain movements. The ancient "nei tan" alchemists strived to produce and store dynamic vital forces in the body, in order to be able to deploy them at will. Here are the roots of T'ai Chi Chuan. Taoism adopted the notion of prolonging life from the "nei tan" alchemists and integrated it into a philosophy and a religion. In the ongoing dynamic process between the primary forces Yin und Yang, Taoism had already integrated the principle of transformation. Thus, contrary to the Christian theologians and alchemists in Europe, hardly any area of conflict existed in China between Taoists and alchemists.

Both types of alchemy, the internal and the external, relied on symbols in order to describe the processes of internal and external transformation. This is where animals and their characteristics entered the picture. The transformation of the snake into a bird was well known. The snake, also portrayed as a dragon or salamander, is transformed into a bird, through its confrontation with the elements, earth, water, air and fire. If the alchemistic process culminates in the liberation of the essence of life, it means that one could move in space as freely as a bird in flight. The snake and the bird symbolize the space between heaven and earth.

The human being stands upright between these poles. While gravity is drawing the body downward toward the earth, the character of the spirit seems to be striving upwards, like the bird, toward an ethereal sphere. Movement happens within this dynamic context. Knowing that, one day, the body will return to the ground, generates a need to believe, as it is promised in so many religions, that something will live on. Thus, the "soul", the primary life force, ascends, flies "upwards" toward "heaven".

That all cultures see the life process, from cradle to grave, as a transformation is evident in their rituals. These differ from one culture to another. T'ai Chi Chuan is also a ritual. It has a fixed structure and its contents are rooted in Taoism and "nei tan" alchemy. Although much of this knowledge has been lost in our times, the fascination of the ritual itself continues. And it evidently affects body and mind. T'ai Chi Chuan proceeds entirely pragmatically on the assumption, that since training, on a regular basis, serves health, it prolongs life. It should, in any case, improve the quality of living. Physical relaxation augmented by breathing and slow movements affects feelings and thoughts. Fixations give way as perspectives widen. This can be experienced as a creative transformation process of one's own person.

The alchemists could not have access to the knowledge available today through brain research and psychology. But they did foresee some kind of connection between physical and psychic processes. External alchemy worked in the laboratory, internal alchemy worked with the human body. Both sought insights about the fundament of all life.

Today, this research is delegated to science. Nevertheless, everyday life engenders transformation processes affecting body and mind that are deeply moving. Like the snake, one must glide through the depths of existence in order to emerge, like a golden rooster, with a new insight about life. Its golden feathers stand for those moments, in which one has recognized something essential. This fulfilling recognition is happiness.

Reach for the seven stars

This second reference to stars in the long form of T'ai Chi Chuan concerns the sevens stars of the Big Dipper, a constellation that has had great significance in most cultures of the Northern Hemisphere. It is at the center of myths that gave a higher meaning to the observer's understanding of existence.

The Big Dipper is so impressive a constellation, because it circles the North Star, and is always visible in the northern sky.[24] It's location is found by following the band of light of the Milky Way against the darker zones of the sky, where the lighter stars burn brighter making their constellations more evident. The way that points of light against a darker background relate to each other prompts perception to automatically seek known figures in the way they interrelate. In this way, the mind puts unknown aspects of the universe in order. The constellations were, thus, identified and named by associating them with familiar, everyday objects.

The names are often in themselves strongly symbolic. Black slaves in the American south referred to the Big Dipper as the Gourd. Their gospel song, "Follow the Drinking Gourd", was a shared secret, a coded plead to be able to escape to the north and freedom. Hunters referred to the Big Dipper as the Bear. Farmers referred to it as the Plough. Merchants and soldiers saw it as a Wagon. Cooks called it a Pot.

At the court of the Emperor of China the government was symbolized in the seven stars and the immobile North Star at the center of the constellation stood for the emperor, around whom the whole universe revolved. A Chinese tale explains the location of the North Star as the dwelling of the Heavenly Ruler, who drives around his realm in a large wagon.[25] The fact that the North Star was visible throughout the entire year, was felt to be proof of the ruler's omnipresence and his everlasting meaning for the entire world.

The North Star, which is the only star in the sky that does not move, is the cardinal point of the north. Myths ascribed force and power to its location. Germanic culture, like the Chinese, also saw this location as the residence of the gods. In the ancient worldview of the Chinese the earth was a four-cornered disk. Pillars in each corner supported the arch of the sky, and a World Tree or Ladder toward Heaven in the center was the axis connecting it to earth. The K'un-lun mountains are found in the middle of this realm, and since the central axis between heaven and earth was supposedly located there, as well, it remained to be explained why the star, around which everything revolves, is not also found above the center, too, but in the far north.

The ancient myths propose traditional explanations. One version recounts how the goddess Nü Wa saved the universe from the destruction of imminent chaos.[26]

As a sister of the Heavenly Emperor she was the mender of marriage, laid down marriage laws, regulated matchmaking as well as the relations between marriage partners. After her brother's death, she took over the government. A man, named Gung Gung was, however, not at all agreed to this, and, overestimating himself, bitterly opposed the new empress. He used a magic spell to cause rivers to overflow their banks, bringing the country and its inhabitants in grave danger. Nü Wa commanded the god of fire to end this catastrophe. Gung Gung lost the battle and, in a fit of rage, hit his head against a mountain in the northwest, breaking one of the pillars that supported the sky. It inclined and, in the southwest, the earth and the sky separated. The earth had lost a great deal of its substance, and, in order to save it, Nü Wa mended the sky with melted, five-colored stones and directed the great flood toward the east into the sea. Then, she created supports for the four corners of the earth with the four legs of a giant turtle.

This myth offers an explanation of why the northern point of the compass hangs so low above the horizon. The cardinal directions played a significant role in Chinese culture. The North Star was the seat of the divinity, which endowed earthly rulers with his power. Temples, palaces and government buildings were also constructed to allow the ruler, as a representative of the highest divinity, to look out from the north toward the south, while the commoners, of course, had to look from the south toward the north.

T'ai Chi Chuan maintains the motif of the directions that refer to the cardinal points. Interestingly enough, the long form begins and ends with the whole body facing north, – an obvious reference to the ancient Chinese customs of orientation and thought.

The image, "Reach for the seven stars" comes up shortly before the end of the long form. In her interpretation of T'ai Chi Chuan as an allegorical journey through life, Gerda Geddes refers to the Taoist belief, that a wise person is flown on the back of a crane to the seven stars, when life comes to an end. When a taoistic wise man had achieved total control over his energies, Ching, Ch'i und Shen, he was, according to belief, supposedly able to determine the time of his own death all by himself. He could now "ride the tiger".

"Reaching for the seven stars" signifies that one's own goal, i.e. the conclusion of the process has been sighted, acknowledged and with it, the end of the path.

Pluck the lotus flower

Why is the beauty of the lotus flower so fascinating? What is beauty? Psychology explains, as mentioned before, that the brain organizes all sensual impressions categorically into figure and background. The conscious mind organizes those impressions that seem to interrelate into a so-called "gestalt" or figure. Regular, symmetrical structures, like the shapes of flowers with their ordered petals, seem to result from an inner coherence that represents harmony and beauty. Psychology refers here to a "good figure", one that is desirable because its orderly appearance apparently creates a feeling of well-being.

In many cultures flowers stand for an absolute perfection, that seems more or less unattainable through the acts of humankind. Nature, or a supposed divinity, is presumed to have the power to engender such perfection. The lotus flower has become a symbol of unblemished purity. Although it roots in the mud, its leaves and blossoms never become soiled. And since the petals are also water-repellent, they are more or less well protected from fungi and other harmful organisms. This physiological immunity associates understandably with notions of perfection, absolute harmony, pure light, all-embracing love and fulfillment. The vital yearning for these qualities is corroborated in pictures, stories or religious texts that are codified in every culture. In life one does not, however, only meet up with "good figures". There is also disharmony, illness, and suffering. These make the sight of a lotus flower all the more impressive.

C. G. Jung did in-depth research on the correlation of symbols and the development of the psyche. In many cultures, as well as in the dreams of his patients, he came upon depictions in which flowers like the rose or the lotus function as the vehicles of the mysteries of life, the realm of the gods, and the matrix of the creation. The basic structures of mandalas resemble the lotus flower. Jung introduced mandalas therapeutically, with agitated patients. Creating a mandala brought order and calm. Indeed, a healing influence is often ascribed to things that are especially beautiful.

Various forms of meditation aim at attaining unusual states of consciousness. Those who meditate work, through exercise, toward a state of mind often described as "untroubled, infinitely calm and unperturbed, peaceful, filled with love". In eastern religions the lotus flower has come to symbolize such ideal states. Chinese alchemy also refers to "the golden blossom" as the essence of life. In a small treatise from the 18th century, "The Secret of the Golden Flower", (Tai I Gin Hua Dsung Dschï)[27], also translated as "The Art of Long Life", the lotus flower, i.e. "the Golden Flower" is compared to light, the divine, the absolute. Lucidity is required in order to uncover the secret of incomparable beauty. Deep calm and careful concentration can give some idea of what is meant by the supernatural. The little book contains instructions for meditation, which supposedly promote the discovery of the secret of life.

T'ai Chi Chuan traditionally pursues images and symbols found in ancient Chinese writings. Each moment of the process, from the start to finish of the long form, turns on the question of practice. There is no short cut to "Conclusion". The exercise requires a clear head, calm, a deepened awareness of physical and mental processes and, above all, this process must be approached from the heart, i.e. with one's entire person. Executing the long form is an "action" performed in order to arrive at "non-action", i.e. in order to recognize and experience new perspectives. Changes of this type can also be measured in the brains of people who are meditating. During meditation the region of the brain in which the psychophysical ego experiences of the momentary surrounding space are located is inactive, while that part of the frontal lobe that processes momentary information one is highly aware of, is especially active. This means for the ego: acting is making way for insight.

The image of the lotus flower appears at the end of the long form, "Ride the tiger and pluck the lotus flower". It is the zenith of human life experience. Gaining complete control over one's energies permits access to an extraordinary experience, and that widens perspectives immeasurably. The euphoric dissolution of boundaries, as well as a feeling of complete security accompanies the discovery of the lotus flower's secret. Without losing its sense of identity, the ego now participates in something felt to be greater than itself. The lotus flower is plucked, becoming one's personal property. This recognition is experienced as a personal belonging that can never be taken away. In Zen it is referred to as the moment of enlightenment.

The greatest potency is ascribed to that, which is extraordinarily beautiful. Who would not wish to be a part of this?

Shoot the golden arrow

The time has come. The lotus flower is plucked. A new level of recognition has been attained: one has understood something about all-embracing love. The old Taoist can now relinquish life and set out his soul on the path toward the gods. With this goal in mind, he can "shoot the golden arrow". Whenever gold appears in the long form, it is an alchemistic synonym for the essence of life, and knowledge about what is vitally essential. When shooting an arrow the archer is capable of a total concentration on the immediacy of his existence, which he can relinquish when his consciousness arrives at the zenith of its completeness. His thoughts are not aiming on the target – the location of the gods –; they are focused instead on the wholeness of his integrated vital forces. He can relinquish these now, for he is convinced that, in such a state of consciousness, the arrow will, hit the target without fault. In other words, the archer is capable of being totally present in the Here and Now. Although the target is right before his eyes, the process itself of arching the bow and shooting the arrow is more important. This process must be experienced with utmost clarity.

The long form devotes itself here to a long breath, in order to permit the experience of calm to intensify the total awareness of the moment. If one is entirely present, one can "let go" entirely and keep going. For a moment, time seems to stand still. A bit of eternity is in the air.

Gerda Geddes associates the image of archery with the experience of dying. A 2000 year old urn bearing the image of a Chinese archer[28] dating back to about B.C. 100 to the Western Han dynasty seems to confirm that it symbolizes the moment of death. The merry facial expression of the archer is particularly striking. The eyes seem to be gazing inwardly and outwardly at the same time, the body is completely tensed, the center of gravity is grounded, and the posture resembles the basic posture in T'ai Chi Chuan. The way the archer seems to bond with the ground gives him the necessary stability to achieve perfect balance and release the arrow with the assurance that he is going to hit the target.

How does this symbolization of the final passing relate to everyday life? There are several parallels. One is repeatedly in the process of working on something that, when finished, will be abandoned as one goes on to the next thing. After a meal is cooked, it is brought to the table. All preparations cease, for there is nothing more to be done, the food is put on the table to be eaten. Or, after having worked a long time on a project, when it is unveiled, the work is over. And one lets go of it.

There is more. Letting go of something is not always the result of a conscious decision. Everything perceptible is subject to passing time, and time does not stand still. Human existence in space and time counteracts holding on; one must let go of each passing moment. This implies, that, without even being aware of it, every millisecond of existence resembles a process of letting go. In reality, it is not yet clear how time proceeds.

The fact, that time does pass, is mirrored in the way living things and objects change. The sun, moon and stars change their positions daily, as they have been doing for millions of years. Over thousands of years, mountains are slowly worn away by wind and water. The blossom on a fruit tree becomes an apple, which can, after maturing for weeks, also go bad within a few days. A vacation that was taken long ago can come to mind in the present accompanied not only by feelings that are attached to it, but also by the memory of certain scents. It is possible to think ahead into the future and imagine, how the world might look twenty years from now. Fantasies about the past and the future can be experienced so intensively, that they seem to be really happening in the very moment they are being imagined. What epoch is this? What is reality? Is it the past, the future or the momentary process of imagination? These questions remain, in fact, unanswered. The health of the psyche, however, requires, that the mind construct a clear framework in order to assure, that one doesn't get lost while leaping around in thought from one time to another. This is why humankind began to measure time in the first place. With the help of calendars and clocks, the phenomenon of time can be conceived and confirmed. Nonetheless, it is good to remember that all imaginings concerning time are only constructs that aim at bringing order to the chaotic plenitude of changes that mark human existence.

Eastern meditation techniques cultivate the experience of time, by calling for complete attentiveness to every passing moment. These are measured through a breath, a mantra or a movement. This technique can only succeed when a passing moment is abandoned after it has been experienced, in order to enable the next one to be experienced. This awareness training cultivates a heightened mindfulness for all life processes. The onset of each moment has importance. The one is followed up by another, and yet another and so on, and so forth. Relinquishing the previous moment enables the freshness of the present moment to be experienced as important. Relating this to the idea of "shoot the golden arrow" implies, that all processes in human existence will always arrive at a conclusion and an opportunity to "shoot the golden arrow". This particular point of view invokes a feeling of lightness and timelessness. The creativity researcher, Mihaly Csikszentmihalyi refers to this phenomenon as "flow", a psychic state describing a "happiness" or "contentment" that results from abandoning oneself completely to the moment at hand.

The long form of T'ai Chi Chuan culminates through a dense and forceful succession of movement images, charting a mystical path that leads to the culmination of life. First, however, the snake has to slide down into the water once again. Submerging into the unconscious is prerequisite to the process, in which the various forms of energy achieve final transformation. With closed fists, as a sign of the will to have made the ultimate decision, one reemerges and turns toward the seven stars. One is now prepared to put one's soul in the hands of heaven. Stepping back, to "ride the tiger" one prepares for the final journey. Then "the crane spreads its wings", i.e. the crane is ready to embark on the great flight that will bring the soul to the seven stars. Having merged all the forms of energy in a totality of life experience, one "rides the tiger". This is the moment of total clarity, the recognition of all-embracing love that enables one "to pluck the lotus flower". Afterwards, with one long breath and great calm, one "shoots the golden arrow" and the body releases the soul.

Shooting the golden arrow implies that one releases one's soul in order to place one's life at disposal. And what happens then? Is one going to live on among the gods? Will one be born again? And what are the implications for everyday life here? The self-understanding of ancient Eastern religions showed people the possibility of offering their abilities to the world, for example, through reincarnation. The veracity of this notion cannot be investigated, for it is a question of belief. Everyday existence, however, can be investigated. Here, an Eastern understanding can help one to develop a new set of ethics rooted in the principle, that personal abilities be put in the service of mankind, again and again.

In the long form of T'ai Chi Chuan the movement figure, "shoot the golden arrow" leads into familiar movements: "pivot – ward off and box – push – carry the tiger to the mountain". This symbolizes the fact that life goes on, enriched now by the consciousness of a new, all-embracing experience and insight. These can become a part of daily existence. According to Lao-tse mankind is continually in a process of entering and leaving life. In this procedure one puts the abilities that have been developed at the disposal of the world. One does not rest on the laurels of things one "has", but devotes oneself to "being". One is manifest as the person one is through the things one does, and the things one has. Stopping here would, however, imply stagnation. Taoism is based on a dynamic, cyclic world view, and view of mankind. This dynamic cycle is designated as "Tao", the path.

Conclusion

The long form is completed. The hands are folded and the position of the arms forms a circle. The feet are in a closed position, side by side. The movement of the encircled arms traces a half-circle away from and in front of the body. The movement ends in a bow. The arms sink, the feet stride, parallel to one another, in order to assume the same body position as at the very beginning. The cycle is complete. This ending implies a new beginning.

Here, the basic tenet of Eastern philosophy is symbolized in body move-ment. Having passed through a dynamic life cycle, one can now, like a re-incarnation, begin all over again. Viewed from this perspective repetition makes sense. In order to be able to execute the succession of movement figures again, the final position mirrors the beginning position.

Within this cycle each part of the long form, as the previous chapters have shown, incarnates a particular life quality. Connecting the symbols to their corresponding movements stimulates the reflection of vital issues. Thus, thought becomes movement and movement engenders thoughts.

T'ai Chi Chuan concretizes the ideology of Taoism. Idea and thought are incorporated, and then materialize through movement. T'ai Chi Chuan offers an experience of the proximity of spirit and matter, that are not separate, but unified. In its materialization through the body, spirit is given a form of expression. And physical experience offers access to spiritual insight.

In the brain the proximity of body and mind is particularly dense. Although images, words, and movements are processed in different regions of the brain, they are networked in a myriad of ways. The interrelation of word, symbol image, imagination, breath and movement undergo an intensive training in T'ai Chi Chuan. Their association establishes particular movement programs. As a result, the movements themselves will evoke the conscious awareness of their respective names, symbols and contents. This training in networking fosters the experiential unity of body and mind.

In all cultures, mysticism thematizes holistic experience. Such experiences are only accessible through intensive training. The interpretation of mystical experience depends entirely on the imagination and spiritual tenets that preoccupy those who have them. If one contemplates the long form of T'ai Chi Chuan as a representation of existential processes and experiences the cyclical character of its succession of movement figures, one has probably come very close to a mystical experience of the Taoistic view of the world.

Continual processes of change are connected to the experience of emptiness and fullness. Transformation is a movement of the mind (thoughts, imagination and feelings) and matter (the body). This dynamic interchange evolves, as designated in the taoistic symbol of Yin and Yang, within the circle of the movement path. One experiences each movement figure as discrete, limited, finite. The phenomenon of change itself, however, is experienced as never-ending, limitless, and infinite.

The circular movement itself has a beginning and an end, like an individual life, limited or finite. The circular movement path itself, however, has no beginning and no end, is limitless, infinite. Moving along this limitless path every moment is like a mere station that infers continuation. In other words, that which is finite infers that which is infinite, and that which is infinite infers that which is finite. Since both insights are experienced simultaneously, they are not experienced as a contradiction, but as a whole. The boundaries of the body, of feeling and of thinking are, for a moment, suspended, resulting in a feeling of deep happiness.

This type of experience does not play a central role in T'ai Chi today, for civil society has distanced itself from religiosity. It is also quite possible to practice T'ai Chi purely as physical training, and enjoy its benefits as such. Its relaxing effect and its positive influence on health become quickly evident in a variety of ways. Correlating this physical exercise with the additional contents of Taoism and associating the results to one's own life experience offers an opportunity for personal change in terms of feelings, thoughts and actions. Relating the philosophical, psychological and spiritual contents of T'ai Chi Chuan into an everyday context awakens new and different perspectives, than those usually available to the Western mind.

The analytic Western world-view is unable to conceive holistic experience with ease. Although Christian mysticism has been well acquainted with this training path, the church never particularly supported it, for mystical thought generally finds any notion of power questionable. To anyone who experiences the unity of body, mind and spirit from within and without, from above and below, hierarchies will always play a secondary role. Hierarchies are by nature inconstant, for they are, as all life forms, inherently subject to change.

Holistic experience of the unity of body and mind offers the insight, that a change is but a limited moment of reality that always passes, i.e. relinquishment is constant, infinite. This has implications regarding the conception of identity: The singularity of the individual ego is felt to be something relative, that can also be experienced as part of something greater than one's own person. In the same way, the perception of reality as something limited can be lived as the awareness of a momentary station on a never-ending, circular path of infinity. The quality of time can, thus, be experienced simultaneously as something limited and momentary, as well as limitless and infinite.

The final movement, "Conclusion", offers insight into the momentary character of life processes, as well as their implications of infinity. The closing bow embodies thankfulness for an existence that enables the experience of this wholeness as a premonition of the fulfillment of transformation.

References

[1]   Photos of a burial object from B.C. 168 in which two figures are portrayed doing Taoistic health gymnastics. Painting on silk. In: Needham, Joseph. (1983). 156.

[2]   40 images of gymnastic exercises were found and documented in a drawing. Ibid. 157.

[3]   Ibid. 156 f.

[4]   Western worldview is well portrayed in a woodcut by Flammarion: „Der neue Mensch durchbrach die begrenzte Welt des ptolemäischen Universums und erblickte neue Wunder." In: Teichmann, Jürgen. (1983). 230.

[5]   Courtois, Michel. (1968). 151.

[6]   Brecht, Bertold. (1981).

[7]   This text can be read in: Anders, Frieder. (1985).148.

[8]   The original story can be found in: Walls, Jan und Yvonne. (1984). 1 f. The exact numbers are of religious-scientific interest. They are found in many Chinese fairy tales and myths. Measuring demonstrates that an attempt is being made to control the uncontrollable. Large numbers, for example, supposedly grasp and limit the concept of unimaginable timeframes and distances.

[9]   Reproduction in: Christie, Anthony. (1968). 49.

[10]   A very differentiated analysis of the parallels between myths and child development with reproductions of children's drawings can be found in: Bischof, Norbert. (1996).

[11]   www.liufangmusic.net/English/pipa_song.html.

[12]   On this website there are photos of the Pipa virtuoso, Liu Fang, in extreme concentration. An example of mindfulness: www.mondomix.com/archives/theatredelaville/2005/liufang/liufang-reportage.htm Galerie.

[13]   Eliade, Mircea. (1975). 419.

[14]   The original fable can be found in: Wilhelm, Richard. (1921). 27 f. Chinese fabels often end with an explanation of the story. Here the narrator steps out of the tale, forcing the listener or reader to assume a reflective, detached attitude.

[15]   In this reproduction, a pair of ancient Chinese vases are being held by monkeys. Their eyes are large, alert, and seem to be taking in everything around them. In: Christie, Anthony. (1968). 123.

[16]   The Pali-Kanon, the holy writings of the Buddhists in Sri Lanka, Burma and Siam, containing the oldest Buddhistic teachings, draws on ancient, mythical images. One passage draws a parallel between human consciousness and monkeys that are jumping about. In: Grunow. A. (1965). 109.

[17]   Schiller, Friedrich von. Der Taucher. In: Echtermeyer. (1966). 280 ff.

[18]   A shortened form of the story can be found in: Geddes. (1991). 58.

[19]   For more detailed questions see Schwarzer, Ralf. (1992). 28 f.

[20]   A striking image of a bronze figure of a wild horse in: FitzGerald, Patrick. (1975). 84.

[21] The Jade Maiden is portrayed in an image in: Wilhelm, Richard. (1921). Picture I. Myth Nr. 16. 37 ff. In German the star myth Nr. 135 can be found in Normann. Friedrich. (1925). 396 ff. Also see the remarks on myth 135 in: Normann. 490, in which a verse from an ancient Chinese calendar is cited.

[22] Myth 2 corresponds to myth Nr. 136 in: Normann, Friedrich. (1925). 399 ff.

[23] Reproduction of alchemistic work: The search for primal matter, the basic principle of life. A transformational process. In: Jung, Carl Gustav. (1990). 391.
Commentary on the reproduction: The work of the alchemists with the retort: The pigeon rises out of the four elements: terra = earth, aqua = water, aer = air, ignis = fire. It symbolizes the spirit liberated from matter. The salamander, also often depicted as a dragon or snake, symbolizes the primal body, that can transform itself by passing through the four elements. This passage results in a specific bird, a pigeon, a pheasant or a golden rooster as a symbol of the spirit.

[24] The Big Dipper circling the North Star. Reproduction in: Widmann, W. und Schütte K. (1968). 10.

[25] Chinese reproduction from 147 A.D.: a relief from Wu-liang-tse entitled "The Wagon of the Ruler". The Big Dipper is portrayed as a wagon carrying the Heavenly Ruler, that is surounded by supplicants. A high official and his attendants are approaching in order to pay their respects. In: Normann, Friedrich. (1925). 236 and 504: cited source: Chavannes, Mission archéologique dans la Chine septentrional. Paris 1890, 65 – 73.

[26] Myth in: Jockel, Rudolf. (1953). 222 f.

[27] Description of the golden flower in: Wilhelm, Richard. (1929). 101 ff. C. G. Jung wrote the commentary to this book and added mandalas, that were painted by patients. Plate 1, 69, depicts a "golden flower, the most beautiful of all flowers".

[28] The photograph of the 2000 year old clay urn with the archer is by Stephen Selby. (1998). See: www.atarn.org/letters/letter_summaries.htm. 1st picture: "Painting on a western Han pottery urn." Ca. B.C. 100.

Literature

The following list evolved during the course of many research projects. This book draws on all these sources. The list is arranged according to specific fields. There is also interdisciplinary overlapping.

Personal research relating to T'ai Chi Chuan

Buser-Rüther, Theresia. (1994). Chinesische Schöpfungsmythen. Deutungsperspektiven in Psychologie und Religionswissenschaft. Psychologische und religionswissenschaftliche Forschungsarbeit. Universität Zürich.

Buser-Rüther, Theresia. (1995). T'ai Chi Chuan and Alchemy. The human quest for transformation within wholeness. Religionswissenschaftliche Forschungsarbeit. Universität Zürich.

Buser-Rüther, Theresia. (1995). Konzepte in der Kreativitätsforschung. Psychologische Forschungsarbeit. Universität Zürich.

Buser-Rüther, Theresia, Stirnimann-Baldegger, Ruth. (1996). „Gegenwelt" als bewusstseinsveränderndes Moment am Beispiel der Meditation und des Chaoskonzeptes. Religionspsychologische Forschungsarbeit. Universität Zürich.

Buser-Rüther, Theresia. (1997). Meditationsformen. Ein religionspsychologischer Vergleich. Forschungsarbeit mit Perspektiven aus den Neurowissenschaften, der Psychologie und der Religionswissenschaft. Universität Zürich.

T'ai Chi Chuan practice

Anders, Frieder. (1985). T'ai Chi Chuan. Meditation in Bewegung zur Steigerung des Körpergefühls und zur Festigung der Gesundheit. Düsseldorf: Econ.

Chungliang Al Huang. (1988). Tai Ji. In der Bewegung zu Harmonie und Lebensfreude finden. Einführung und Anleitung. Gräfe und Unzer.

Da Liu. (1987). T'ai Chi Ch'uan and Meditation. London: Routledge & Kegan Paul.

Geddes, Gerda. (1991). Looking for the Golden Needle. An allegorical journey. Plymouth: Mannamead Press.

Geddes, Gerda. (1995). Die Suche nach der Goldenen Nadel. Eine allegorische Reise durch das T'ai Chi Chuan. Wien: Verlag Publication PN° 1 Bibliothek der Provinz. Übersetzung der 2. überarbeiteten Auflage von Looking for the Golden Needle.

Liang, T.T. (1974). T'ai Chi Chuan for health and self-defense. Boston.

Li Ding, Bambang Sutomo. (1988). Taiji Qigong Twenty-Eight Steps. Beijing: Foreign Languages Press.

Lie, Foen Tjoeng. (1987). Chinesisches Schattenboxen. Tai-Ji-Quan für geistige und körperliche Harmonie. Niedernhausen/Ts.: Falken-Verlag.

NRK. (1989). The Magic bird spreads its wings. A Programm about T'ai Chi Ch'üan and Pytt Geddes. Video.

Schatz, Hilmar. (1986). T'AI CHI CH'UAN – das chinesische Schattenboxen. München: TR-Verlagsunion.

Video Martial Arts International. (1989). Understanding T'ai Chi Ch'üan. Long Yang Form, performed by Gerda Geddes. Video Beckmann Communications.

ohne Autor. (1990). Simplified "Taijiquan". China Sports Series I. Beijing: China Sports Editorial Board.

ohne Autor. (1991). Competition Routines for four Styles Taijiquan. Beijing: People's Sports Publishing House of China.

Yu Shenquan. (Ed.). (1991). Yang Style Taijiquan. Beijing: Morning Glory Publishers.

Neuro-science and medicine:
Fundamentals relating to diverse forms of meditation

Davidson, Julian A., Davidson, Richard J. (Eds.). (1980). The psychobiology of consciousness. New York: Plenum Press.

Decety, J., Jeannerod, M., Durozard, D., Baverel G. (1993). Central activation of automatic effectors during mental simulation of motor actions in man. Journal of Physiology, 461, 549 – 563.

Delmonte, M. M. (1985). Meditation and anxiety reduction: A literature review. Clinical Psychology Review, 5, 91 – 102.

Dittrich, Adolf. (1985). Aeriologie-unabhängige Strukturen veränderter Wachbewusstseinszustände. Stuttgart: Ferdinand Enke Verlag.

Dittrich A., Arx, S., Staub, S. (1985). International study on altered states of consciousness (ISASC). Summary of the results. The German Journal of Psychology, 9, 319 – 339.

Dittrich, Adolf, Hofmann, Albert, Leuner, Hanscarl. (Hrsg.). Welten des Bewusstseins. 4 Bände: Band I (1993 a). Ein interdisziplinärer Dialog. Band 2 (1993 b). Kulturanthropologische und philosophische Beiträge. Band 3 (1994 a). Experimentelle Psychologie, Neurobiologie und Chemie. Band 4 (1994 b). Bedeutung für die Psychotherapie. Berlin: Verlag für Wissenschaft und Bildung.

Elias, A. N., Wilson A. F. (1995). Serum hormonal concentrations following transcendental meditation – potential role of gamma aminobutyric acid. Medical Hypotheses, 44, 287 – 291.

Gellhorn, E., Kiely, W. F. (1972). Mystical states of consciousness. Neurophysiological and clinical aspects. Journal of Nervous and Mental Disease, 154, 399 – 405.

Isen, Alice M. (1990). The influence of positive and negative affect on cognitive organisation: some implications for development. In: Stein, Nancy L., Leventhal, Bennett and Trabasso, Tom. (Eds.). Psychological and biological approaches to emotion. Hillsdale, New Jersey: Lawrence Erlbaum Associates Publishers. 75 – 94.

Janowiak, John J., Hackman, Robert. (1994). Meditation and college students' self-actualization and rated stress. Psychological Reports, 75, 1007 – 1010.

Jin, Putai. (1992). Efficacy of T'ai Chi, brisk walking, meditation, and reading in reducing mental and emotional stress. In: Journal of Psychosomatic Research, Vol. 36, No. 4, 361 – 370.

Kabat-Zinn, Jon. (1982). An outpatient program in behavioral medicine for chronic pain patients based on the practice of mindfulness meditation: theoretical considerations and preliminary results. General Hospital Psychiatry 4, 33 – 47.

Kabat-Zinn, J. Lipworth, L. Burney, R. (1985). The clinical use of mindfulness meditation for the self-regulation of chronic pain. Journal of Behavioral Medicine, 8, 163 – 190.

Kabat-Zinn, J. Lipworth, L. Burney, R., Sellers W. (1986). Four-year follow-up of a meditation-based program for the self-regulation of chronic pain: treatment outcomes and compliance. The Clinical Journal of Pain, 2, 159 – 173.

Kabat-Zinn, J., Chapman-Waldrop, A. (1988). Compliance with an outpatient stress reduction program: rates and predictors of completion. Journal of Behavioral Medicine, 11, 333 – 352.

Kabat-Zinn, J. (1990). Full Catastrophe Living: Using the Wisdom of Your Body and Mind to Face Stress, Pain, and Illness. New York: Delcorte.

Kabat-Zinn, J. (1991). Gesund und stressfrei durch Meditation. Das grosse Buch der Selbstheilung. Bern: Otto Wilhelm Barth.

Kabat-Zinn, J., Massion, A. O., Kristeller, J. et al. (1992). Effectiveness of a meditation-based stress reduction program in the treatment of anxiety disorders. American Journal of Psychiatry, 149, 936 – 943.

Kabat-Zinn J. (1993). Mindfulness Meditation: Health Benefits of an Ancient Buddhist Practice. In: Goleman, D., Gurin, J. (Eds). Mind/Body Medicine. Yonkers, NY: Consumer Report Books. 259 – 275.

Kabat-Zinn, J. (1994). Wherever You Go, There You Are: Mindfulness meditation in Everyday Life. New York: Hyperion.

Kandel, E. R., Schwartz, J. H., Jessell, T. M. (Hg.). (1996). Neurowissenschaften. Eine Einführung. Heidelberg: Spektrum Akademischer Verlag.

Kaplan, Kenneth H., Goldenberg, Don L., Galvin-Nadeau, Maureen. (1993). The impact of a meditation-based stress reduction program on Fibromyalgia. General Hospital Psychiatry, 15, 284 – 289.

Kasamatsu, A., Hirai, T. (1966). An Electroencephalographic Study of Zen-Meditation (Za-Zen). Folia Psychiatria et Neurologia Japonica, 20,

315 – 336. Nachgedruckt in: Tart, Charles. (1969). Altered States of Consciousness. New York: John Wiley & Sons.

Koukkou-Lehmann, Martha. (1987). Hirnmechanismen normalen und schizophrenen Denkens. Eine Synthese von Theorien und Daten. Heidelberg: Springer.

Koukkou-Lehmann, M. (1991). Hirnmechanismen der menschlichen Kommunikation und schizophrene Symptomatik. Swiss Med, 13, Nr. 4. 21 – 28.

Koukkou M., Lehmann, D. (1993). A model of dreaming and its functional significance: The state-shift hypothesis. In: Moffit, A., Kramer, M. and Hoffman, R. (Eds.). The functions of dreaming. Albany, N. Y.: State University of New York Press.

MacLean, C. R. K., Walton, K. G., Wenneberg, S. R., Levitsky, D. K., Mandarino, J. V., Waziri, R., Schneider, R. H. (1994). Altered Responses of Cortisol, GH, TSH and Testosterone to Acute Stress after Four Months' Practice of Transcendental Meditation (TM). Annals of the New York Academy of Sciences, Nov. 30, 746, 381 – 384.

Mandell, Arnold, J. (1980). Toward a Psychobiology of Transcendence: God in the brain. In: Davidson, Julian A. and Davidson, Richard J. (Eds.). The Psychobiology of consciousness. New York: Plenum Press. 379 – 464.

Marlatt, C., Pagano, R., Rose, R., Maques, J. (1984). Effects of meditation and relaxation training upon alcohol use in male social drinkers. In: Shapiro, D. und Walsh, R. (Eds.). Meditation: Classic and contemporary perspectives. New York: Aldine. 105 – 120.

Massion, A. O., Teas, J., Hebert, J. R. Wertheimer, M. D., Kabat-Zinn, J. (1995). Meditation, melatonin and breast/prostrate cancer: hypothesis and preliminary data. Medical Hypotheses, 44, 39 – 46.

Miller, John J., Fletcher, Ken, Kabat-Zinn, Jon. (1995). Three year follow-up and clinical implications of a mindfulness meditation-based stress reduction intervention in the treatment of anxiety disorders. General Hospital Psychiatry, 17, 192 – 200.

Newberg, A. B., Iversen, J. (2003). The neural basis of the complex mental task of meditation: neurotransmitter and neurochemical considerations. Medical Hypotheses, 61 (2), 282 – 291.

Pollard, Irina. (2004). Meditation and Brain Function: A Review. Eubios Journal of Asian and International Bioethics 14, 28 – 34.

Roth, Gerhard. (2001). Fühlen, Denken, Handeln. Wie das Gehirn unser Verhalten steuert. Frankfurt: Suhrkamp.

Sawada, Y., Steptoe, A. (1988). The effects of brief meditation training on cardiovascular stress responses. Journal of Psychophysiology, 2, 249 – 257.

Schandry, Rainer. (1988). Lehrbuch der Psychophysiologie. Körperliche Indikatoren psychischen Geschehens. Weinheim: Psychologie Verlags Union.

Schöttler, Ekkehard. (1990). Langzeitwirkungen der Transzendentalen Meditation auf das vegetative Nervensystem. Dissertation. Köln: Hohe Medizinische Fakultät der Universität zu Köln.

Schuman, Marjorie. (1980). The psychophysiological model of meditation and altered states of consciousness: a critical review. In: Davidson, Julian A., Davidson, Richard J. (Eds). The psychobiology of consciousness. New York: Plenum Press. 333 – 378.

Smith, W. Paul, Compton, William C., West, Beryl. (1995). Meditation as an adjunct to a happiness enhancement program. Journal of Clinical Psychology, March, Vol. 51, No 2, 269 – 273.

Störmer-Labonté, Martin, Machemer, Peter, Hardinghaus, Winfried. (1992). Ein meditatives Stressbewältigungsprogramm bei psychosomatischen Patienten. Psychotherapie Psychosomatik medizinische Psychologie, 42, 436 – 444.

Tart, Charles T. (1980). A system's approach to altered states of consciousness. In: Davidson, Julian A., Davidson, Richard J. (Eds). The psychobiology of consciousness. New York: Plenum Press. 243 – 269.

Taylor, Douglas N. (1995). Effects of a behavioral stress-management program on anxiety, mood, self-esteem, and T-cell count in HIV-positive men. Psychological Reports, 76, 451 – 457.

Wallace, Robert Keith. (1970). Physiological effects of Trancendental Meditation. Science, Vol. 167, March, 1751 – 1754.

Wallace, Robert Keith, Benson, Herbert. (1972). The physiology of meditation. Scientific American, February, 84 – 90.

Wang, Youde, Morgan, William P. (1992). The effect of imagery perspectives on the psychophysiological responses to imagined exercise. Behavioral Brain Research. Vol. 52, 167 – 174.

Yue, Guang and Cole, Kelly J. (1992). Strength increases from the motor program: comparison of training with maximal voluntary and imagined muscle contractions. Journal of Neurophysiology. Vol. 67, No 5, May.

Psychology

Binnig, Gerd. (1989). Aus dem Nichts. Über die Kreativität von Natur und Mensch. München: Piper.

Bischof, Norbert. (1989). Das Rätsel Ödipus. Die biologischen Wurzeln des Urkonfliktes von Intimität und Autonomie. München: Piper.

Bischof, Norbert. (1996). Das Kraftfeld der Mythen. Signale aus der Zeit, in der wir die Welt erschaffen haben. München: Piper.

Csikszentmihalyi, Mihaly. (2000). Das flow-Erlebnis. Jenseits von Angst und Langeweile: im Tun aufgehen. Stuttgart: Klett-Cotta.

Frey, Dieter, Gaska, Anne. (1993). Die Theorie der kognitiven Dissonanz. In: Frey, Dieter, Irle Martin. (Hg.). Theorien der Sozialpsychologie. Band I: Kognitive Theorien. Bern: Huber.

Glover, John A., Ronning, Royce R., Reynolds, Cecil R. (Eds.) (1989). Handbook of Creativity. New York: Plenum Press.

Hany, Ernst A. (1993). Kreativitätstraining: Positionen, Probleme, Perspektiven. In: Klauer, Karl Josef. Kognitives Training. Göttingen: Hogrefe Verlag für Psychologie. 189 – 216.

Kebeck, Günther. (1994). Wahrnehmung. Theorien, Methoden und Forschungsergebnisse der Wahrnehmungspsychologie. Weinheim: Juventa Verlag.

Runco, Mark A., Albert, Robert S. (Eds). (1990). Theories of Creativity. Newbury Park: Sage Publications.

Schachter, S., Singer, J. E. (1962). Cognitive, social, and physiological determinants of emotional state. Psychological Review, 69, 379 – 399.

Schwarzer, Ralf. (1992). Psychologie des Gesundheitsverhaltens. Göttingen: Hogrefe.

Sternberg, Robert J. (Ed). (1988). The nature of creativity. Contemporary psychological perspectives. Cambridge: Cambridge University Press.

Tloczynski, Joseph. (1994). A preliminary study of opening-up meditation, college adjustment, and self-actualization. Psychological Reports, 75, 449 – 450.

Science of Religion

Bodde, Derk. (1975). Myths of China. In: Chun-shu Chang. (Ed.). The Making of China. Main themes in premodern Chinese history. London: Prentice Hall International. 5 – 37.

Burkhardt, Helmut, Swarat, Uwe. (1992). Evangelisches Lexikon für Theologie und Gemeinde. Wuppertal: R. Brockhaus.

Cancik, Hubert, Gladigow, Burkhard, Laubscher, Matthias. (Hg.). (1990). Handbuch religionswissenschaftlicher Grundbegriffe. Band 2 Apokalyptik – Geschichte. Stuttgart: Verlag W. Kohlhammer.

Chee Soo. (1986). The Taoist Ways of Healing. The Chinese Art of Pa Chin Hsien. Wellingborough: The Aquarian Press, Thorsons Publishing Group.

Christie, Anthony. (1968). Chinesische Mythologie. Wiesbaden: Emil Vollmer Verlag.

Courtois, Michel. (1968). Die Chinesische Malerei. Lausanne: Editions Rencontre.

Drobin, Ulf. (1982). Psychology, philosophy, theology, epistemology – some reflections. In: Holm, Nils G. (Ed.). Religious ecstasy. Based on papers read at the symposium on religious ecstasy held at Åbo, Finland, on the 26th – 28th of August 1981. Stockholm: Almquist and Wiksell International. 263 – 274.

Dubs, Homer H. (1947). The beginnings of alchemy. Isis. Vol. 38, 62 – 86.

Dunde, Rudolf. (Hrsg.) (1993). Wörterbuch der Religionspsychologie. Gütersloh: Gütersloher Verlagshaus.

Eberhard, Wolfram. (1937). Typen chinesischer Volksmärchen. FF Communications No. 120. Helsinki: Academica scientiarum fennica.

Eberhard, Wolfram. (1942). Lokalkulturen im alten China. Teil 2: Die Lokalkulturen des Südens und Ostens. Untersuchungen über den Aufbau der chinesischen Kultur. II. Peking: The Catholic University.

Eliade, Mircea. (1975). Schamanismus und archaische Ekstasetechnik. Frankfurt: Suhrkamp.

Eliade, Mircea. (1985). Yoga. Unsterblichkeit und Freiheit. Frankfurt: Suhrkamp.

Eliade, Mircea. (Hg.). (1987). The Encyclopedia of Religion. Vol. 3. New York: Macmillan Publishing Company.

Eliade, Mircea. (1992). Schmiede und Alchemisten. Mythos und Magie der Machbarkeit. Freiburg: Herder.

Engel, Klaus. (1995). Meditation. Geschichte, Systematik, Forschung, Theorie. Frankfurt a. M.: Peter Lang.

Fendos, Paul G. (1993). The study of ancient Chinese Myth. Chinese Culture. Vol. 34, No. 1, 31 – 59.

FitzGerald, Patrick. (1975). Das alte China. Luzern: Verlag Kunstkreis Luzern.

Galling, Kurt. (Hg.). (1956). Religion in Geschichte und Gegenwart. Tübingen: J. C. B. Mohr.

Giradot. N. J. (1975/76). The problem of creation mythology in the study of Chinese religion. History of religions. Vol. 15, 289 – 318.

Grimal, Pierre. (1967). Mythen der Völker. Band II. Fischer Bücherei.

Grom, Bernhard. (1992). Religionspsychologie. München: Kösel.

Holm, Nils G. (Ed.). (1982). Religious ecstasy. Based on papers read at the symposium on religious ecstasy held at Åbo, Finland, on the

26th – 28th of August 1981. Stockholm: Almquist and Wiksell International.

Hübner, Kurt. (1985). Die Wahrheit des Mythos. München: Beck.

Jockel, Rudolf. (Hg.). (1953). Götter und Dämonen. Mythen der Völker. Darmstadt: Holle Verlag GmbH.

Johnson, Obed Simon. (1928). A study of Chinese alchemy. Shanghai: The Commercial Press, Limited.

Jung, Carl Gustav. (1988). Vorwort zu Daisetz Teitaro Suzuki: Die grosse Befreiung. GW 11. Olten: Walter.

Jung, Carl Gustav. (1990). Psychologie und Alchemie. GW Bd. 12. Olten: Walter.

Küng, Hans, Ching, Julia. (1988). Christentum und Chinesische Religion. München: Piper.

Lao-tse. (1961). Tao-Tê-King. Das heilige Buch vom Weg und von der Tugend. Übersetzung von Günter Debon. Stuttgart: Reclam.

Martels, Z. R. W. M. von. (Ed.). (1990). Alchemy revisited. Proceedings of the international conference on the history of alchemy at the University of Groningen 17 – 19 April 1989. Leiden: E. J. Brill.

Meadow, Mary Jo, Kahoe, Richard D. (1984). Psychology of Religion. Religion in individual lives. Cambridge: Harper and Row.

Mommaers, Paul. (1996). Was ist Mystik? Frankfurt: Insel Verlag.

Münke, Wolfgang. (1976). Die klassische chinesische Mythologie. Stuttgart: Ernst Klett Verlag.

Naranjo, Claudio und Ornstein, Robert E. (1988). Psychologie der Meditation. Frankfurt: Fischer.

Needham, Joseph. (1979). Wissenschaftlicher Universalismus. Über Bedeutung und Besonderheit der chinesischen Wissenschaft. Frankfurt: Suhrkamp.

Needham, Joseph. (1983). Science and Civilisation in China. Vol. 5. Chemistry and chemical technology. Part V Spagyrical discovery and invention: Physiological alchemy. Cambridge: Cambridge University Press.

Normann, Friedrich. (Hg.). (1925). Mythen der Sterne. Gotha/Stuttgart: Verlag Friedrich Andreas Perthes A.-G.

Ruhbach, Gerhard. (Hrsg.). (1977). Glaube – Erfahrung – Meditation. München: Kösel.

Ruhbach, Gerhard, Sudbrack, Josef. (1989). Christliche Mystik. Texte aus zwei Jahrtausenden. München: C. H. Beck.

Scharfetter, Christian. (1992). Der spirituelle Weg und seine Gefahren. Spiritualität, Begriff, Typen, Bewusstseinsbereiche, Induktoren und Inhalte. Meditation. Spirituelle Krise, Sekten und totalitäre Kulte. Eine Übersicht für Berater und Therapeuten. Stuttgart: Ferdinand Enke.

Sheldrake, Rupert. (1984). Das schöpferische Universum. München: Goldmann.

Sivin, Nathan. (1968). Chinese Alchemy: Preliminary Studies. Cambridge: Harvard University Press.

Sivin, Nathan. (1990). Research on the history of Chinese alchemy. In: Martels, Z. R. W. M. von. (Ed.). Alchemy revisited. Proceedings of the international conference on the history of alchemy at the University of Groningen 17 – 19 April 1989. Leiden: E. J. Brill. 3 – 20.

Stolz, Fritz. (1988). Grundzüge der Religionswissenschaft. Göttingen: Vandenhoek & Ruprecht.

Stolz, Fritz. (2001). Weltbilder der Religionen. Kultur und Natur, Diesseits und Jenseits, Kontrollierbares und Unkontrollierbares. Zürich: Pano Verlag.

Sudbrack, Josef. (1971). Meditation: Theorie und Praxis. Würzburg: Echter.

Sudbrack, Josef. (1988). Mystik. Selbsterfahrung – Kosmische Erfahrung – Gotteserfahrung. Mainz: Matthias-Grünewald-Verlag.

Sundén, Hjalmar. (1982). Religionspsychologie. Probleme und Methoden. Stuttgart: Calwer Verlag.

Teichmann, Jürgen. (1983). Wandel des Weltbildes. Darmstadt: Wissenschaftliche Buchgesellschaft.

Walls, Jan and Yvonne. (1984). Classical Chinese Myths. Hongkong: Joint Publishing Co.

Walters, Derek. (1992). Chinese Mythology. An encyclopedia of myth and legend. London: Aquarian.

Wilhelm, Richard (Ed.). (1921). The Chinese fairy book. New York: Frederick A. Stokes Company Publishers.
Wilhelm, Richard. (1929). Das Geheimnis der Goldenen Blüte. Ein chinesisches Lebensbuch. Zürich: Rascher Verlag.
Wilhelm, Richard. (Hg. und Übersetzer). (1984). I Ging. Das Buch der Wandlungen. Köln: Eugen Diederichs Verlag.
Wörterbuch der Religionen. (1985). Stuttgart: Alfred Kröner Verlag.
Zheng, Chantal. (1989). Mythes et croyances du monde chinois primitif. Paris: Payot.

Diverse forms of meditation

Aitken, Robert. (1995). Zen als Lebenspraxis. Diederichs Gelbe Reihe 78. München: Eugen Diederichs.
Alexander, C. N., Rainforth, M. V., Geldeloos, P. (1991). Transcendental meditation, self-actualization, and psychological health: A conceptual overview and statistical meta-analysis. Journal of Social Behavior and Personality, 6, 189 – 247.
Balthasar, Hans Urs von. (1990). Mein Werk – Durchblicke. Einsiedeln: Johannes Verlag.
Balthasar, Hans Urs von. (1995). Christlich meditieren. Einsiedeln: Johannnes Verlag.
Brantschen, Niklaus. (1991). Erfüllter Augenblick. Meditationen für den Alltag. Zürich: Benziger.
Carrington, Patricia. (1995). Das grosse Buch der Meditation. Bern: Scherz.
Dürckheim, Karlfried Graf. (1993). Meditieren – wozu und wie. Freiburg: Herder Spektrum.
Dumoulin, Heinrich. (1963). Die Zenerleuchtung in neueren Erlebnisberichten. In: Numen 10, 133 – 152.
Dumoulin, Heinrich. (1990). Zen im 20. Jahrhundert. München: Kösel.
Enomiya-Lassalle. H. M. (1995). Zen-Meditation für Christen. Bern: Otto Wilhelm Barth.

Fontana, David. (1994). Kursbuch Meditation. Alles über die verschiedenen Meditationsmethoden und ihre Anwendung. Anleitungen zur Wahl der richtigen Methode. Bern: Otto Wilhelm Barth.

Goleman, Daniel. (1990). Meditation: Wege nach innen. Reihe: Psychologie heute. Weinheim: Beltz.

Griffiths, Paul J. (1987). On being mindless: buddhist meditation and the mind-body problem. La Salle, Illinois: Open Court.

Hirai, Tomo. (1978). Zen and the Mind. Tokyo: Japan Publications.

Huth, Almuth, Huth, Werner. (1990). Handbuch der Meditation. München: Kösel.

Jäger, Willigis. (1982). Kontemplation. Gottesbegegnung heute. Der Weg in die Erfahrung nach Meister Eckehart und der ,,Wolke des Nichtwissens''. Salzburg: Otto Müller.

Jäger, Willigis. (1991). Suche nach dem Sinn des Lebens. Bewusstseinswandel durch den Weg nach innen. Vorträge, Ansprachen, Erfahrungsberichte. Petersberg: Verlag Via Nova.

Kapleau, Philip. (Hrsg.). (1994). Die drei Pfeiler des Zen. Lehre – Übung – Erleuchtung. Bern: Otto Wilhelm Barth.

Lehmann, Karl, Kasper, Walter. (1989). Hans Urs von Balthasar. Gestalt und Werk. Köln: Verlag für christliche Literatur Communio GmbH.

Lotz, Johannes B., S. J. (1973). Kurze Anleitung zum Meditieren. Frankfurt am Main: Verlag Josef Knecht.

Mangoldt, Ursula von. (1966). Meditation und Kontemplation aus christlicher Tradition. Anregungen für alle Suchenden. Weilheim/Obb.: Otto Wilhelm Barth-Verlag.

Nyanaponika, Makatera. (1993). Geistestraining durch Achtsamkeit. Die buddhistische Satipatthana-Methode. Konstanz: Verlag Christiani.

Oezelsel, Michaela M. (1993). 40 Tage. Erfahrungsbericht einer traditionellen Derwischklausur. München: Diederichs.

Raab, Peter. (Hrsg.). (1995). Meditieren – wie und wo. Ein Führer mit 500 Adressen von Lehrern, Häusern und Zentren. Freiburg: Herder.

Satura, Vlasimir. (1981). Meditation aus der Sicht der Psychologie und der christlichen Tradition. Salzburg: Otto Müller.

Schüttler, Günter. (1974). Die Erleuchtung im Zen-Buddhismus. Gespräche mit Zen-Meistern und psychopathologische Analyse. Freiburg: Karl Alber.

Schwäbisch, Lutz, Siems, Martin. (1987). Selbstentfaltung durch Meditation. Eine praktische Anleitung. Reinbek bei Hamburg: Rowohlt.

Sekida, Katsuki. (1993). Zen-Training. Das grosse Buch über Praxis, Methoden, Hintergründe. Freiburg: Herder.

Thomas, Klaus. (1973). Meditation. In: Forschung und Erfahrung, in weltweiter Beobachtung und praktischer Anleitung. Reihe: Seelsorge und Psychotherapie Band 1. Stuttgart: J. F. Steinkopf, Georg Thieme.

Tilmann, Klemens. (1972). Die Führung zur Meditation. Ein Werkbuch 1. Zürich: Benziger Verlag.

Tilmann, Klemens, Peinen, Hedvig-Theresia von. (1978). Die Führung zur Meditation. Christliche Glaubensmeditation. Ein Werkbuch 2. Zürich: Benziger Verlag.

Wissenschaftliche Untersuchungen zur Technik der Transzendentalen Meditation und zum TM-Sidhi-Programm nach Maharishi Mahesh Yogi. Verbesserung in allen Lebensbereichen. (1994). Prospekt.

World Government News. (1978 June). Issue Number 6. Prospekt über die Transzendentale Meditation und das Zentrum von Maharishi Mahesh Yogi.

General and world literature

Brecht, Bertold. (1981). Die Gedichte von Bertold Brecht in einem Band. Frankfurt : Suhrkamp.

Echtermeyer. (1966). Deutsche Gedichte. Von den Anfängen bis zur Gegenwart. Düsseldorf: August Bagel Verlag.

Grunow. A. (1965). Führende Worte. Band IV. Berlin: Haude & Spenersche Verlagsbuchhandlung.

Heug, Sigrid. (1972). Wolkenkind. In: Die Kinderfähre. Stuttgart: Union Verlag.

Widmann, W. und Schütte K. (1968). Welcher Stern ist das? Stuttgart: Franckh'sche Verlagshandlung.

Internet sources

www.atarn.org/letters/letter_summaries.htm: golden arrow

www.China-Kampfkunst.de: „*Shan – der chinesische Fächer*" von Werth,
    Monika: Fan

http://upload.wikimedia.org/wikipedia/commons/6/62/Manuel_Jo-
    seph_2005.jpg: Fan

www.afpc.asso.fr/wengu/wg/wengu.php?l=Tangshi&no=72: Lute

www.chinaservice.de/geschichte.htm: Lute

www.concertlingpipa.ch/d/lingling_yu/pipa.html: Lute

www.liufangmusic.net/cds/solo_albums.html: Lute

www.liufangmusic.net/English/: Lute

www.liufangmusic.net/English/pipa_song.html: Lute

www.mondomix.com/archives/theatredelaville/2005/liufang/liufang-re-
    portage.htm: Lute

www.mondomix.com/archives/theatredelaville/2005/liufang/liufang-re-
    portage.htm Galerie: Lute

www.philmultic.com/German/musik.html: Lute

www.philmultic.com/liufang/interviews/world_music.html: Lute

de.wikipedia.org/wiki/Pipa: Lute

en.wikipedia.org/wiki/Pipa: Lute

CPSIA information can be obtained at www.ICGtesting.com
Printed in the USA
LVOW101253130513

333510LV00016B/326/P